Coloring Book for Baby Boomers

SOUL FULL OF SUNSHINE

Copyright © 2023 by Jo Miller Publishing. All rights reserved. This book or any portion thereof may not be reproduced or used in any manner whatsoever without the express written permission of the publisher.

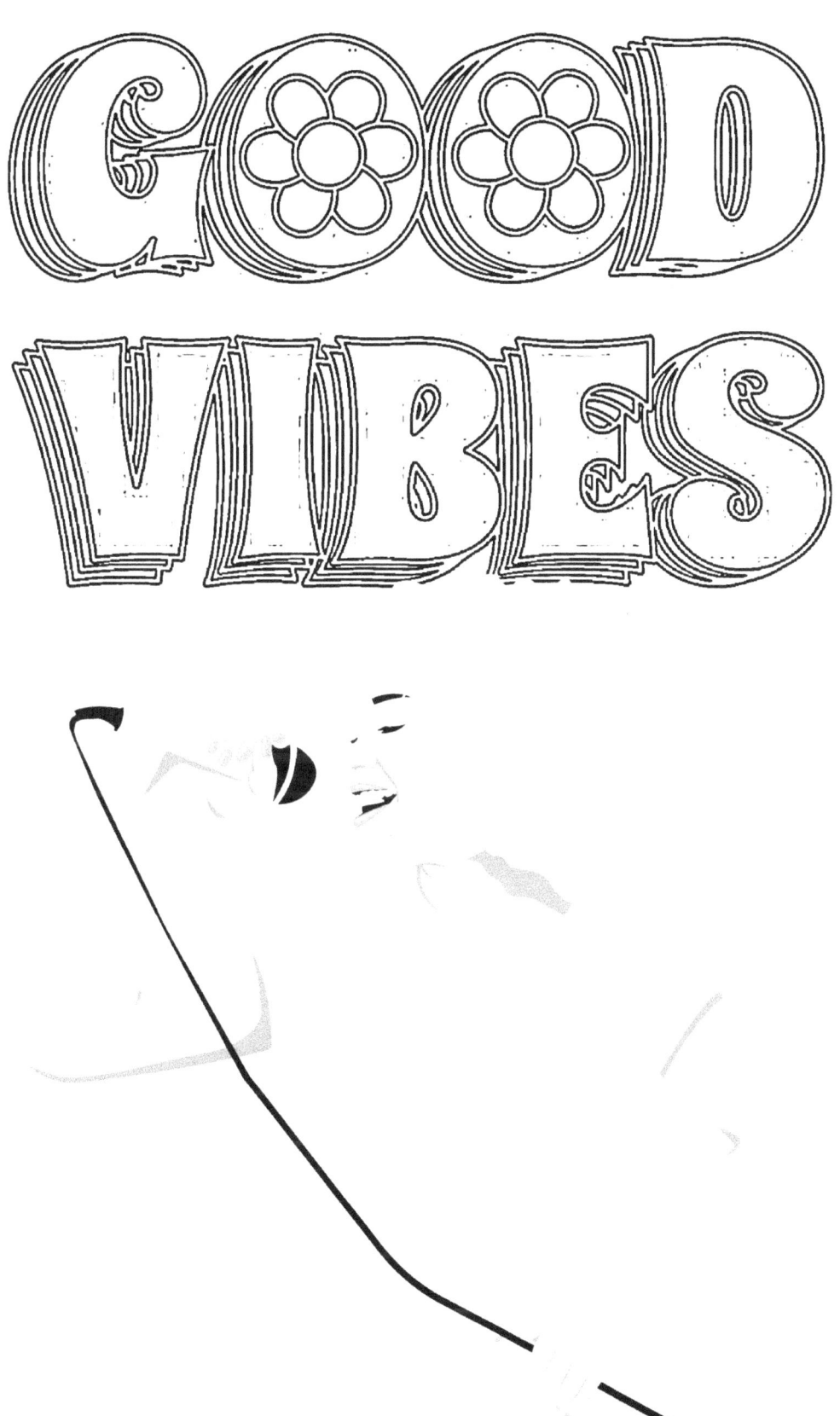

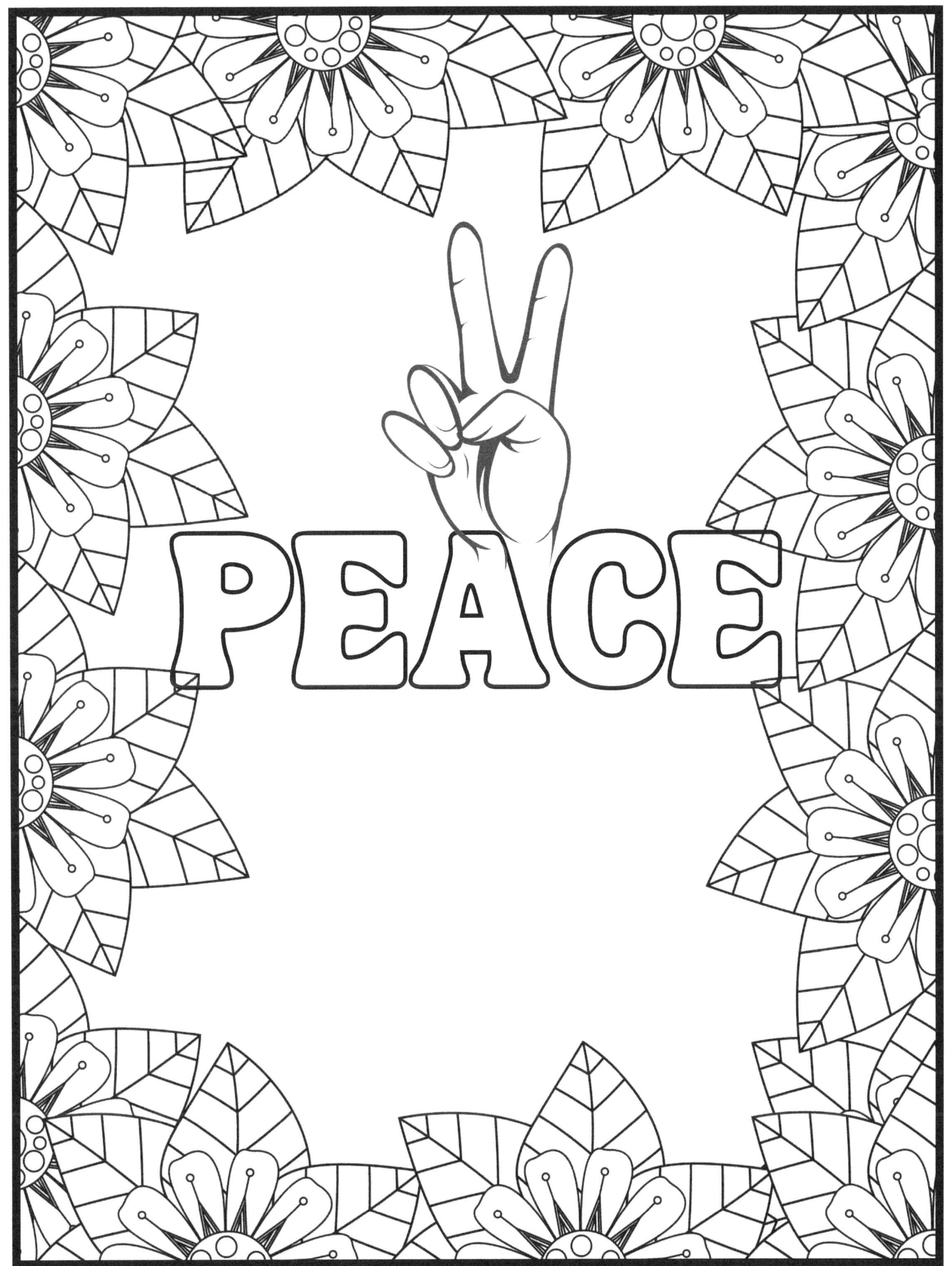

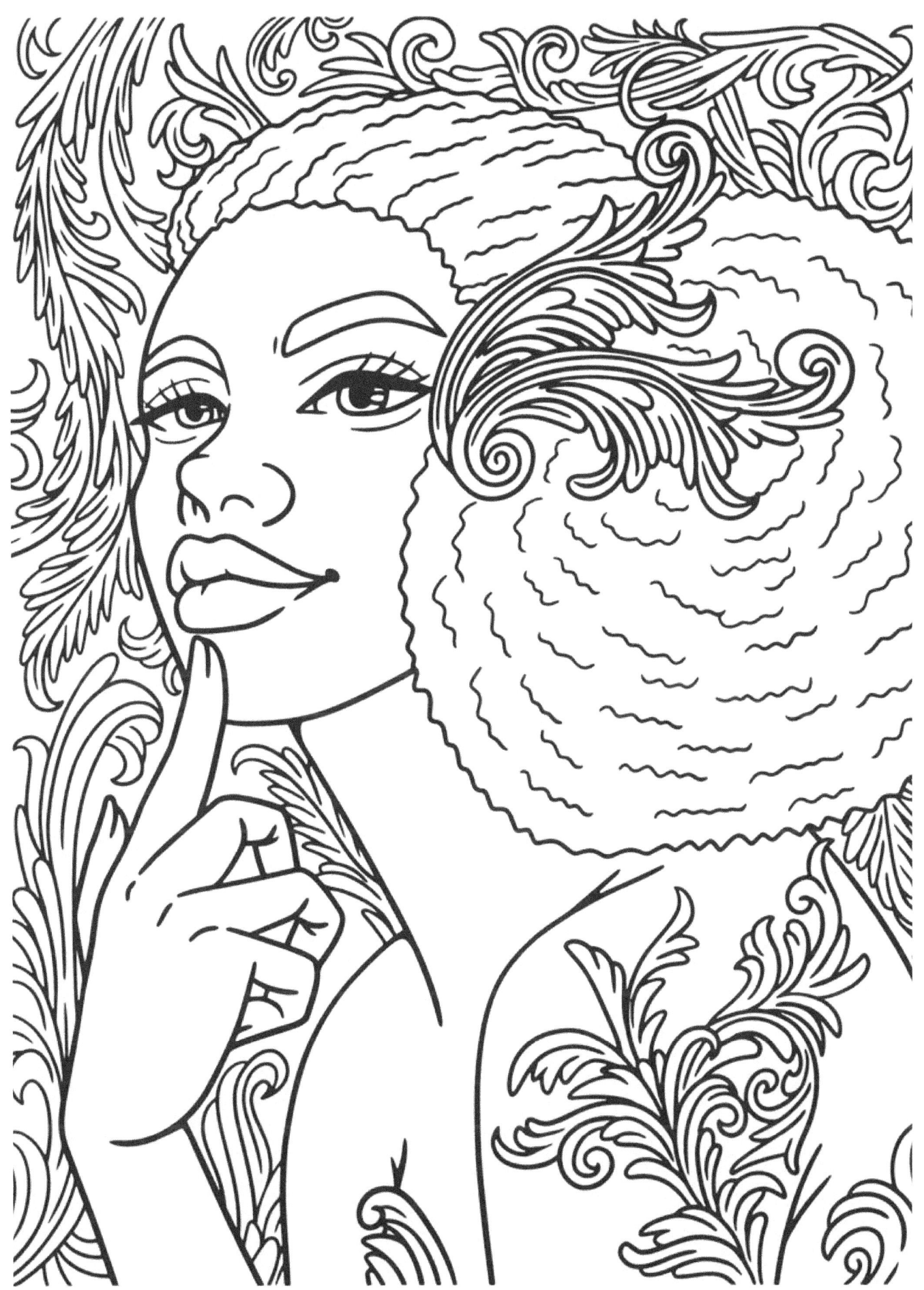

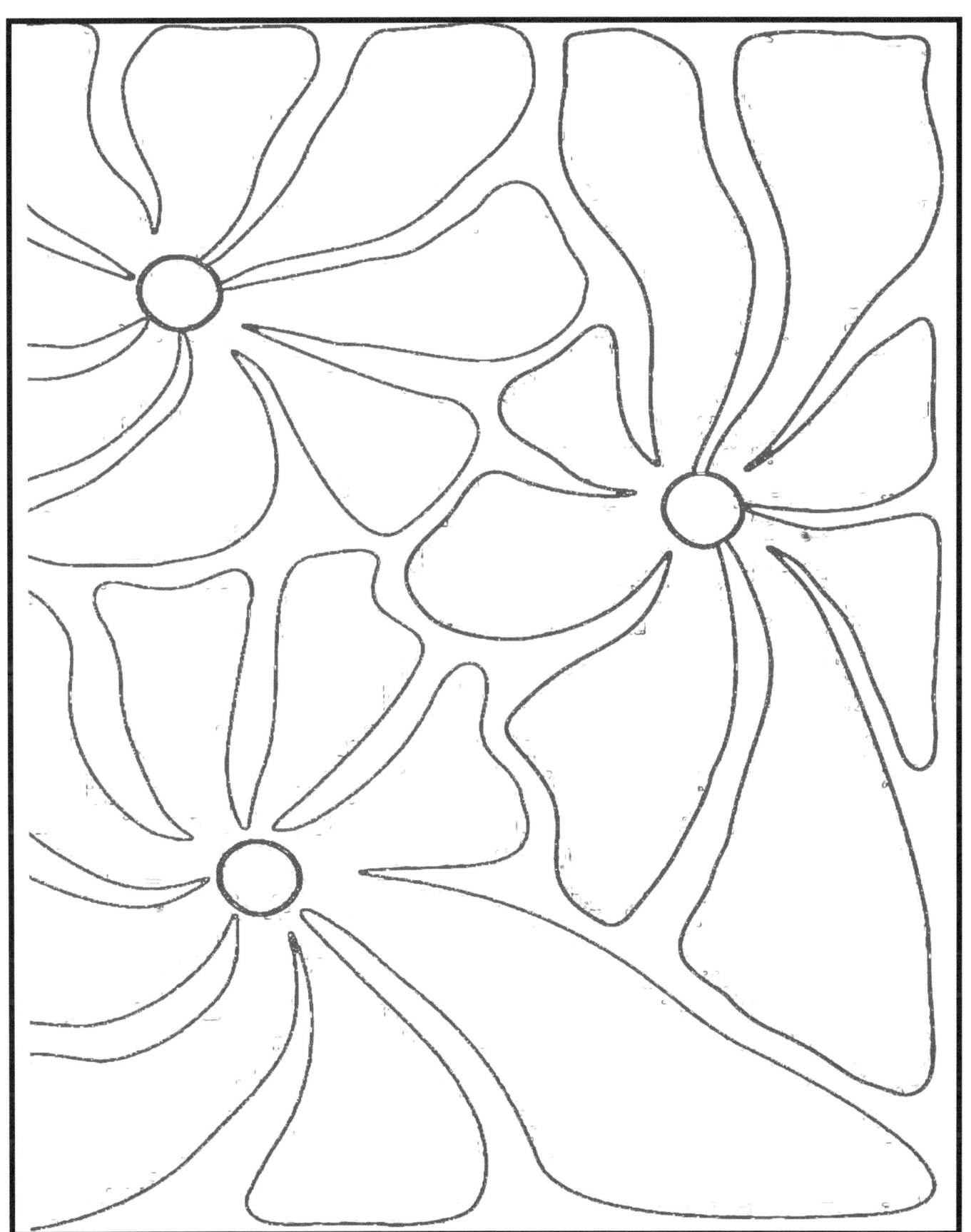

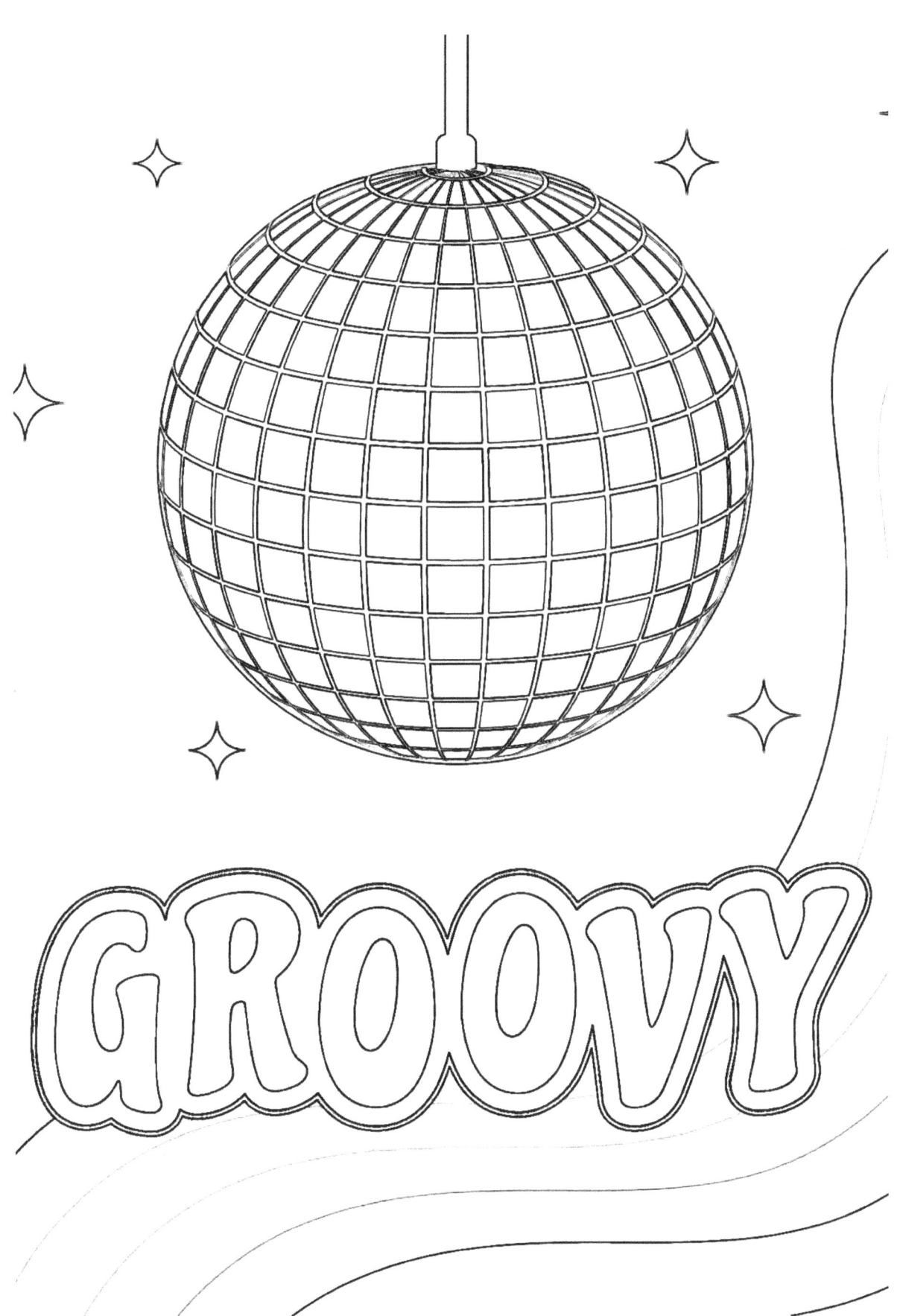

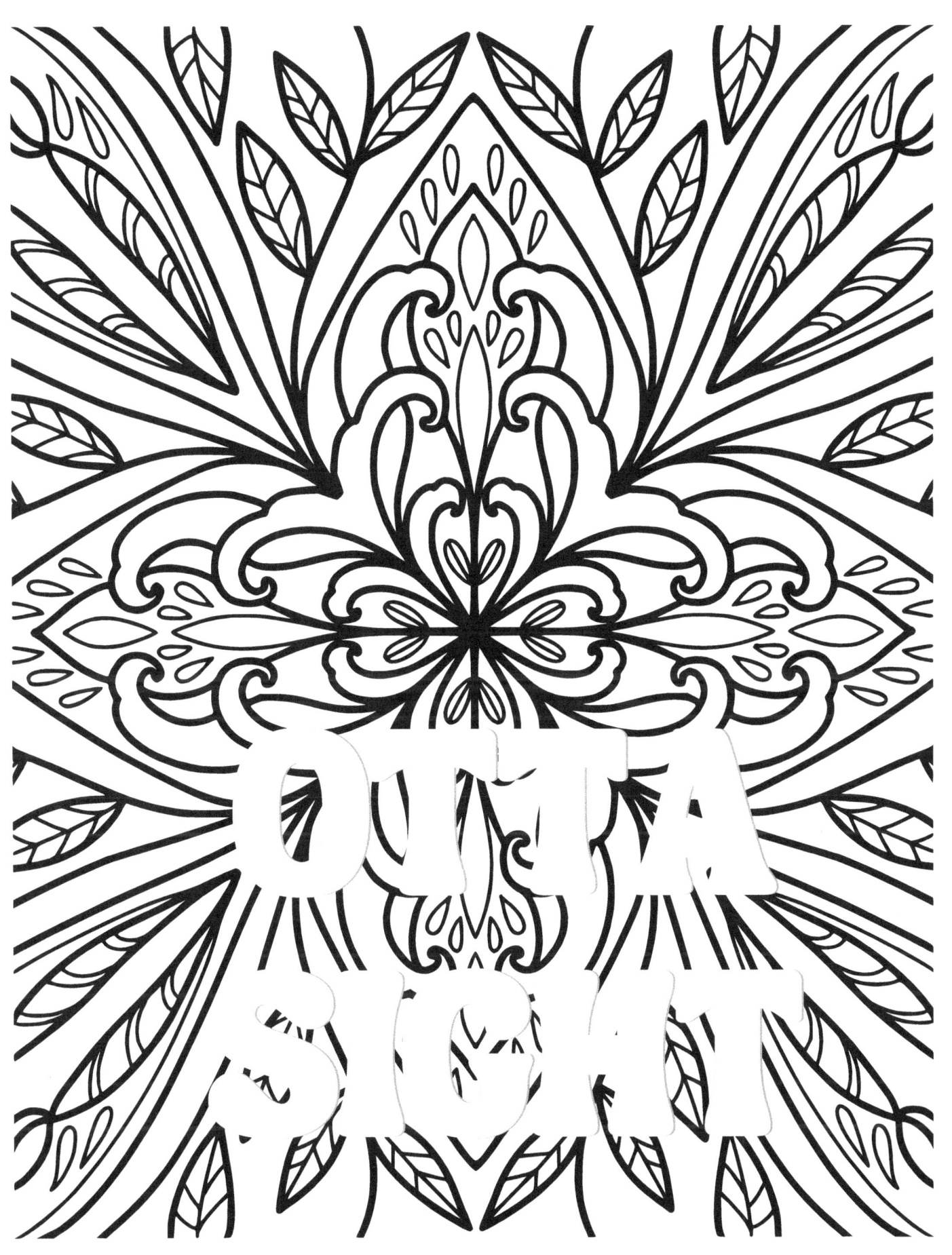

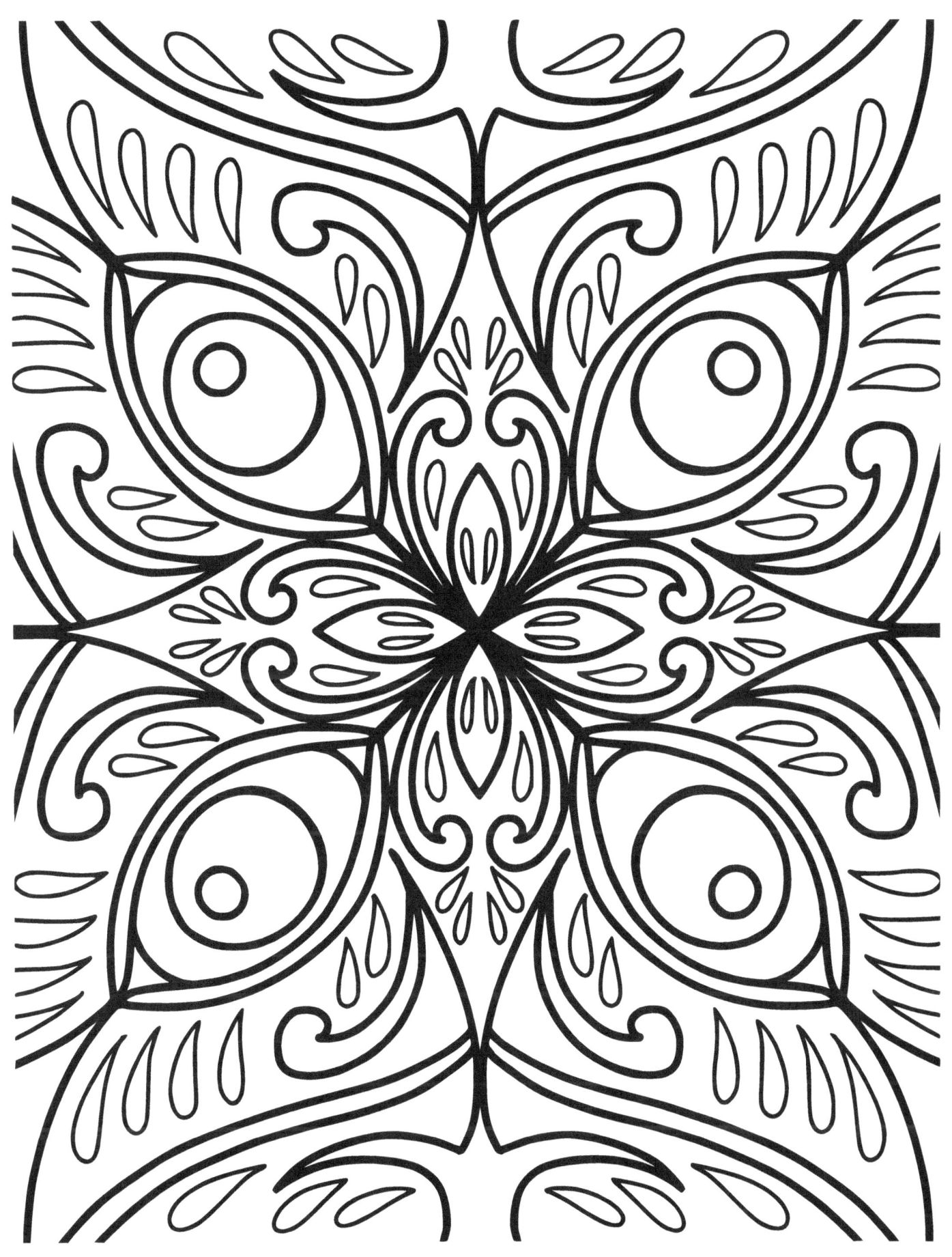

Tie Dye

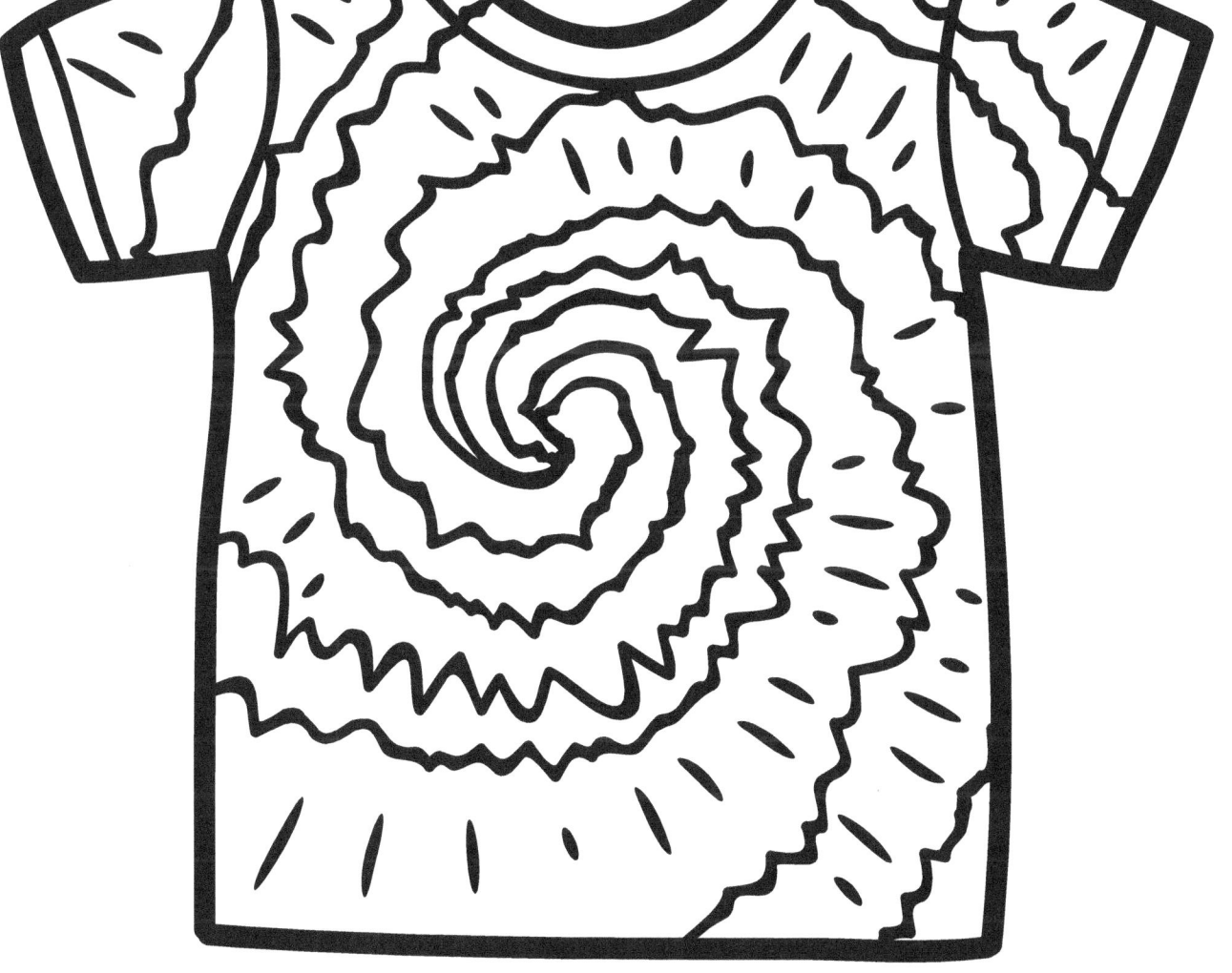

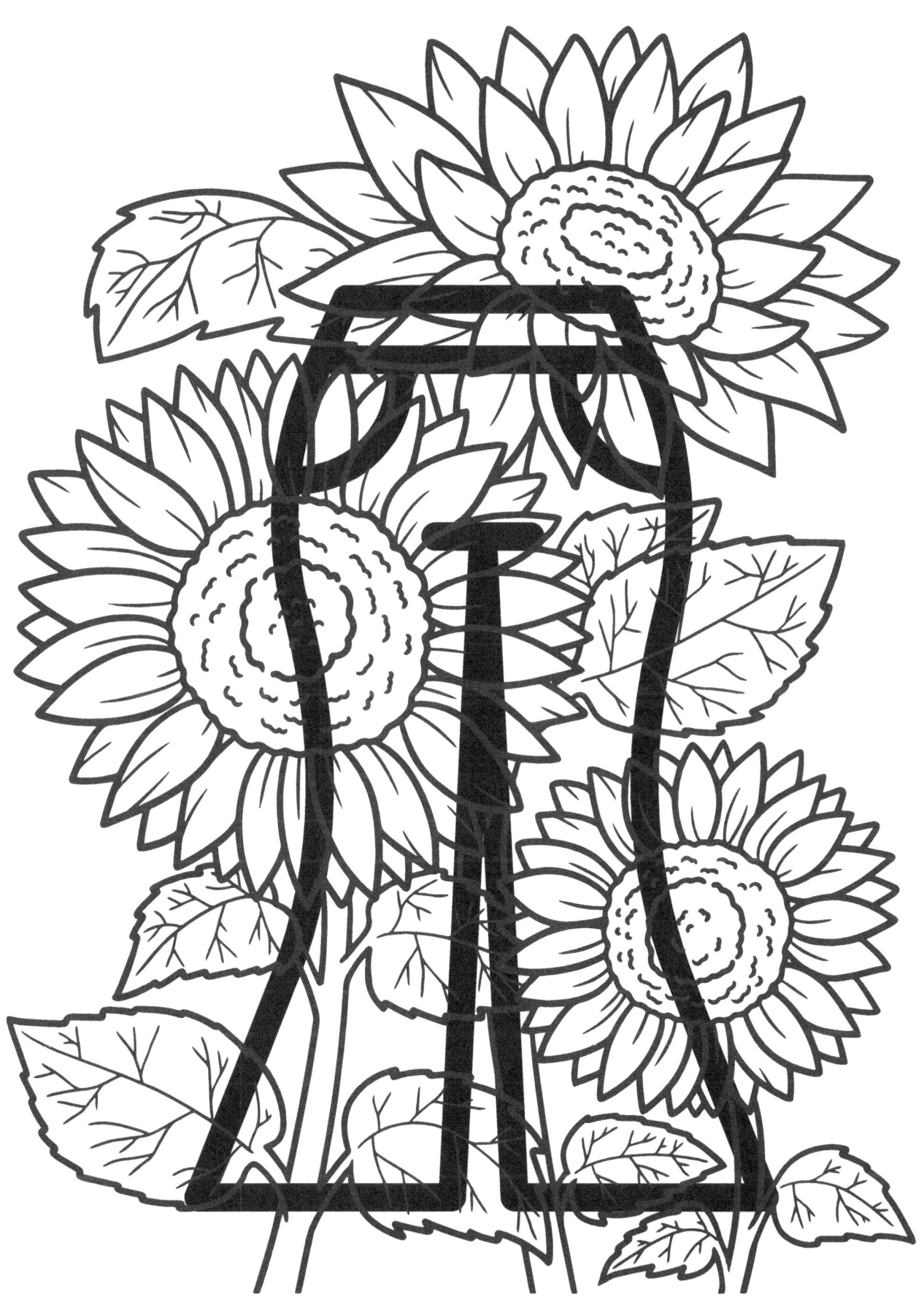

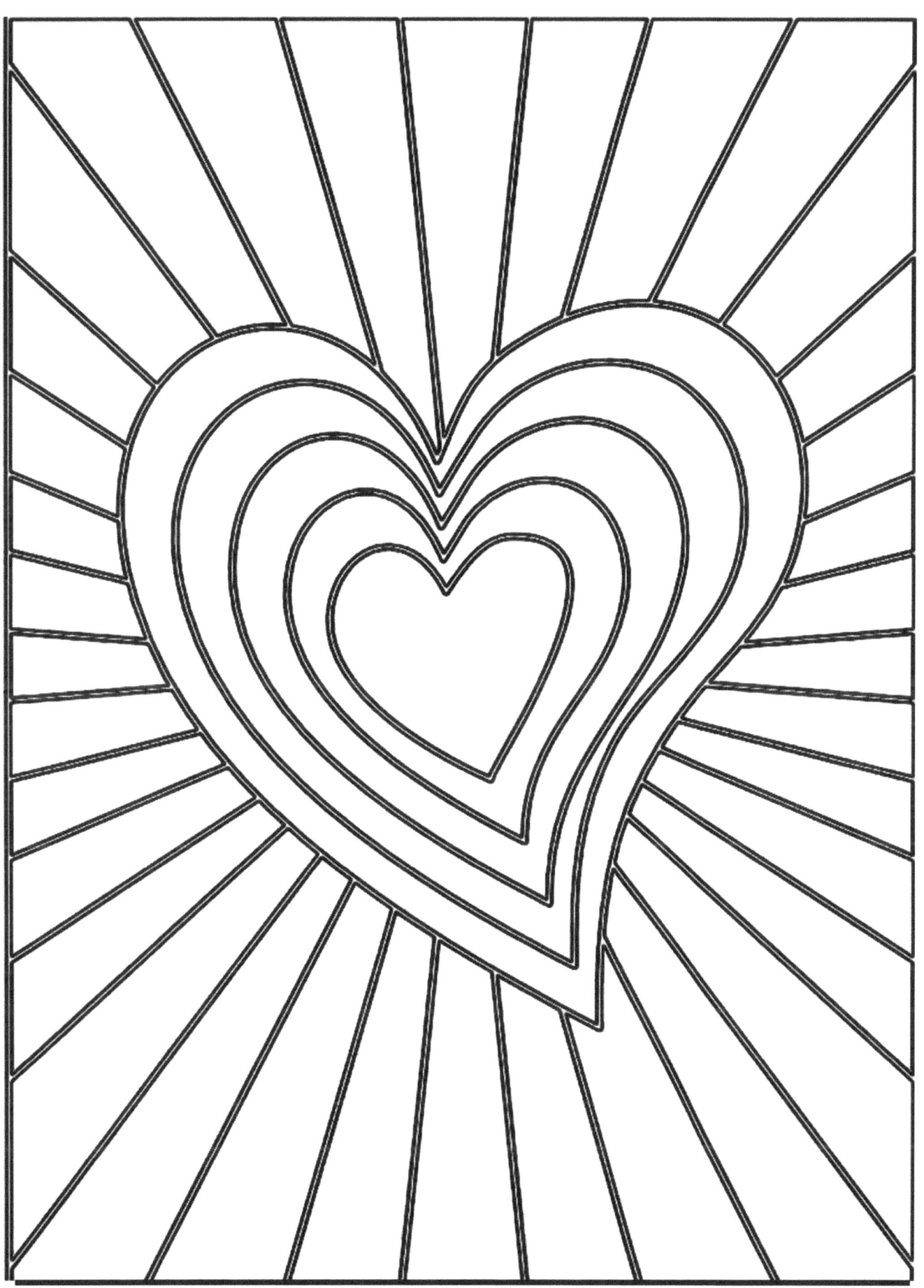

JIVE TURKEY

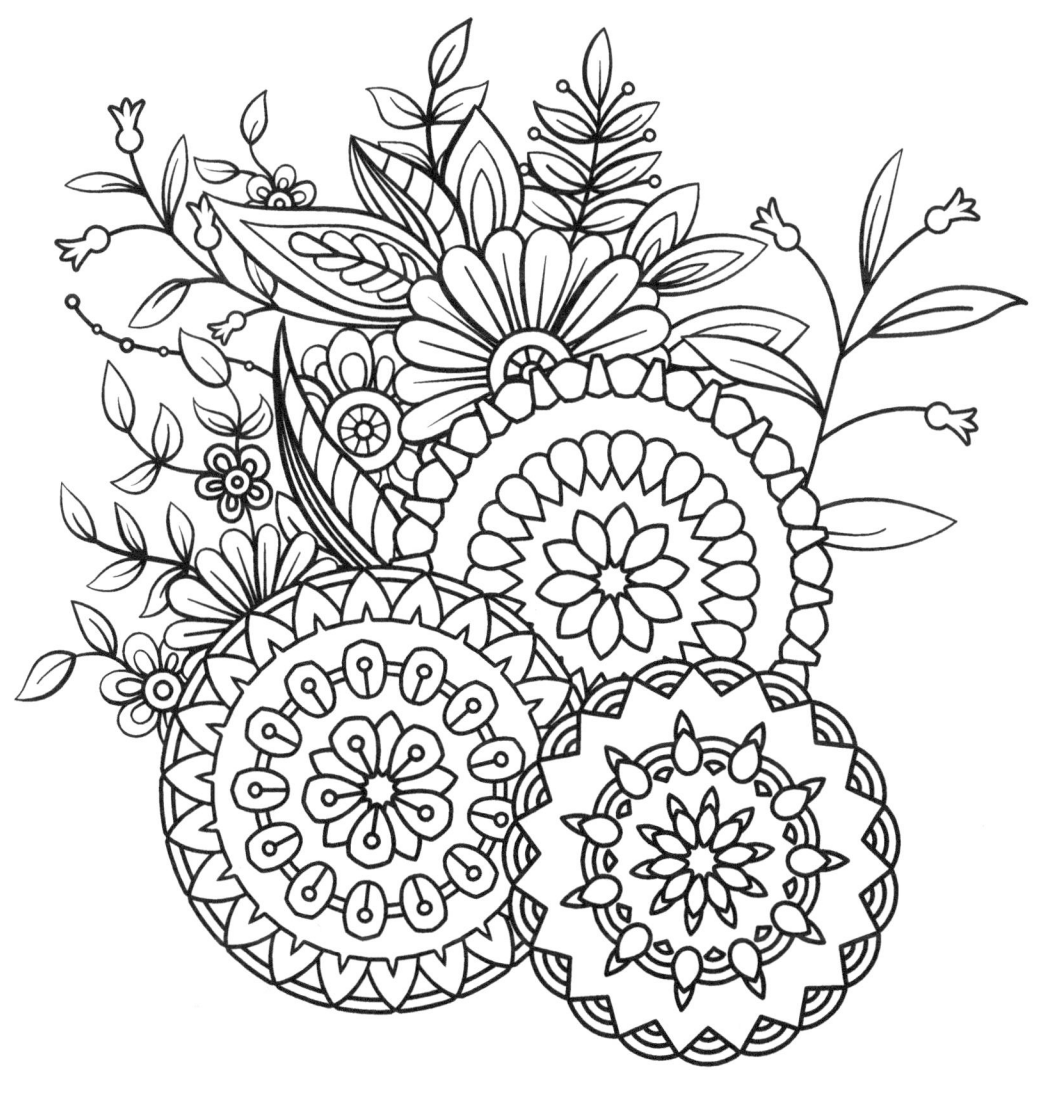

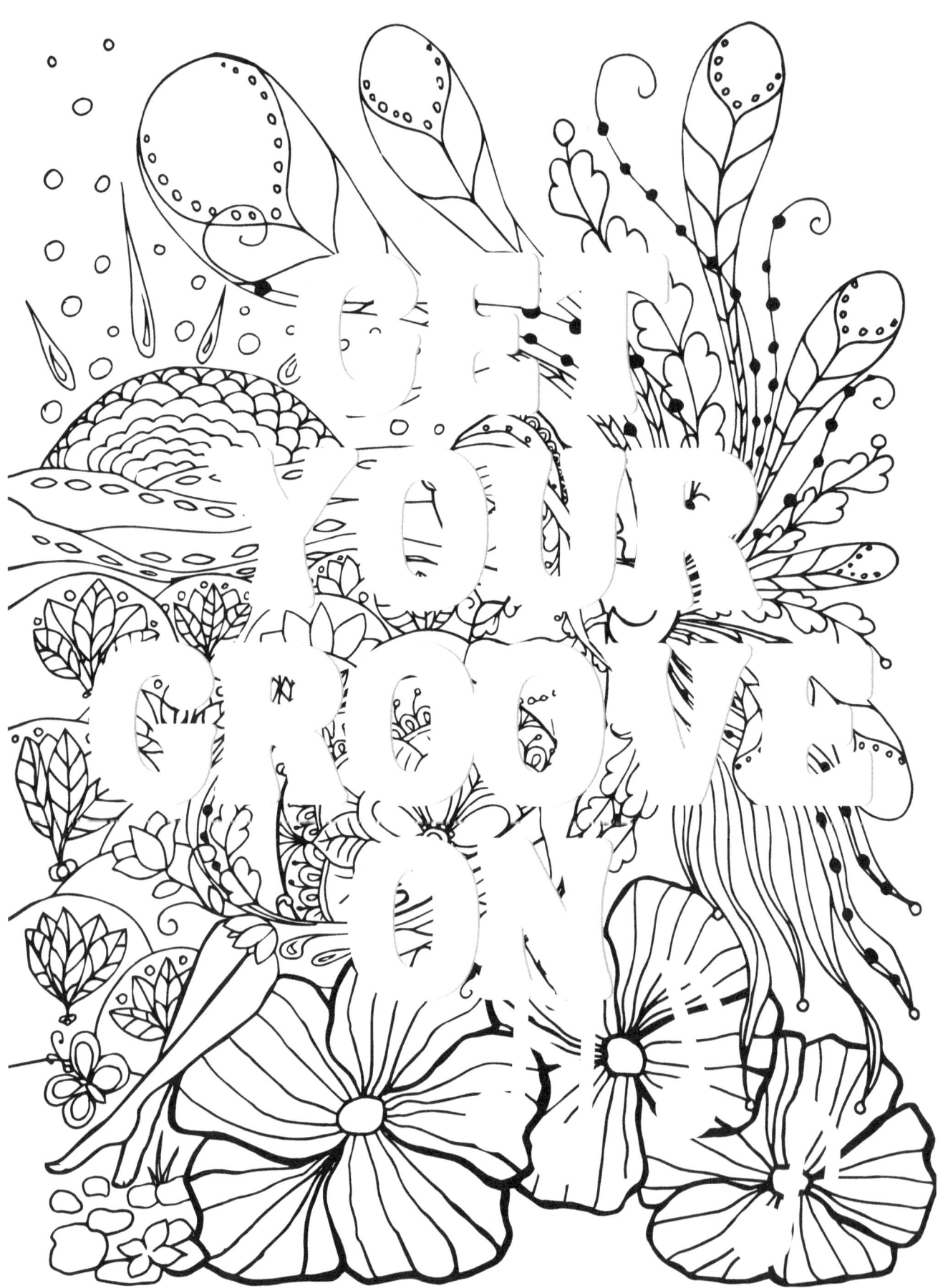

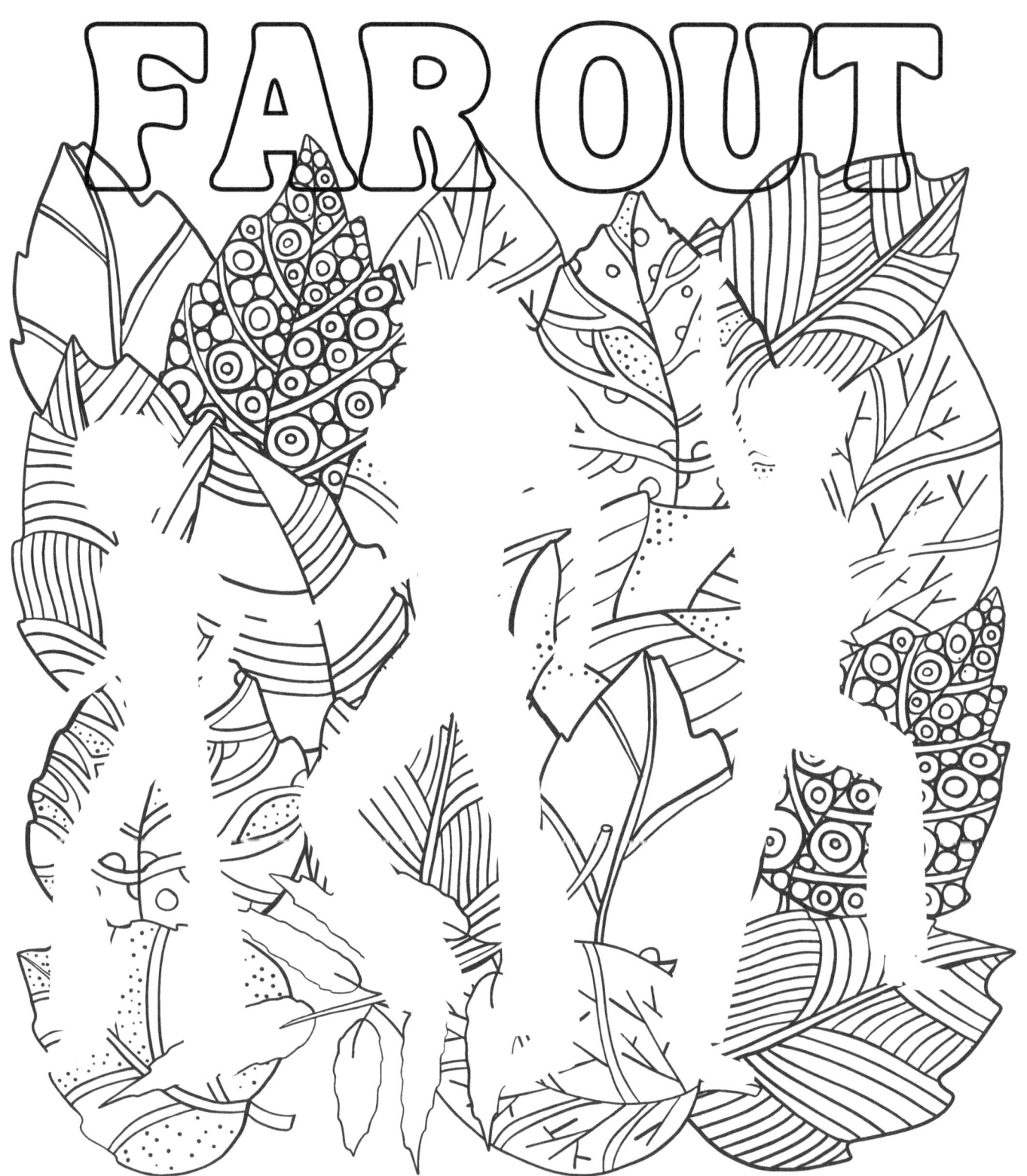

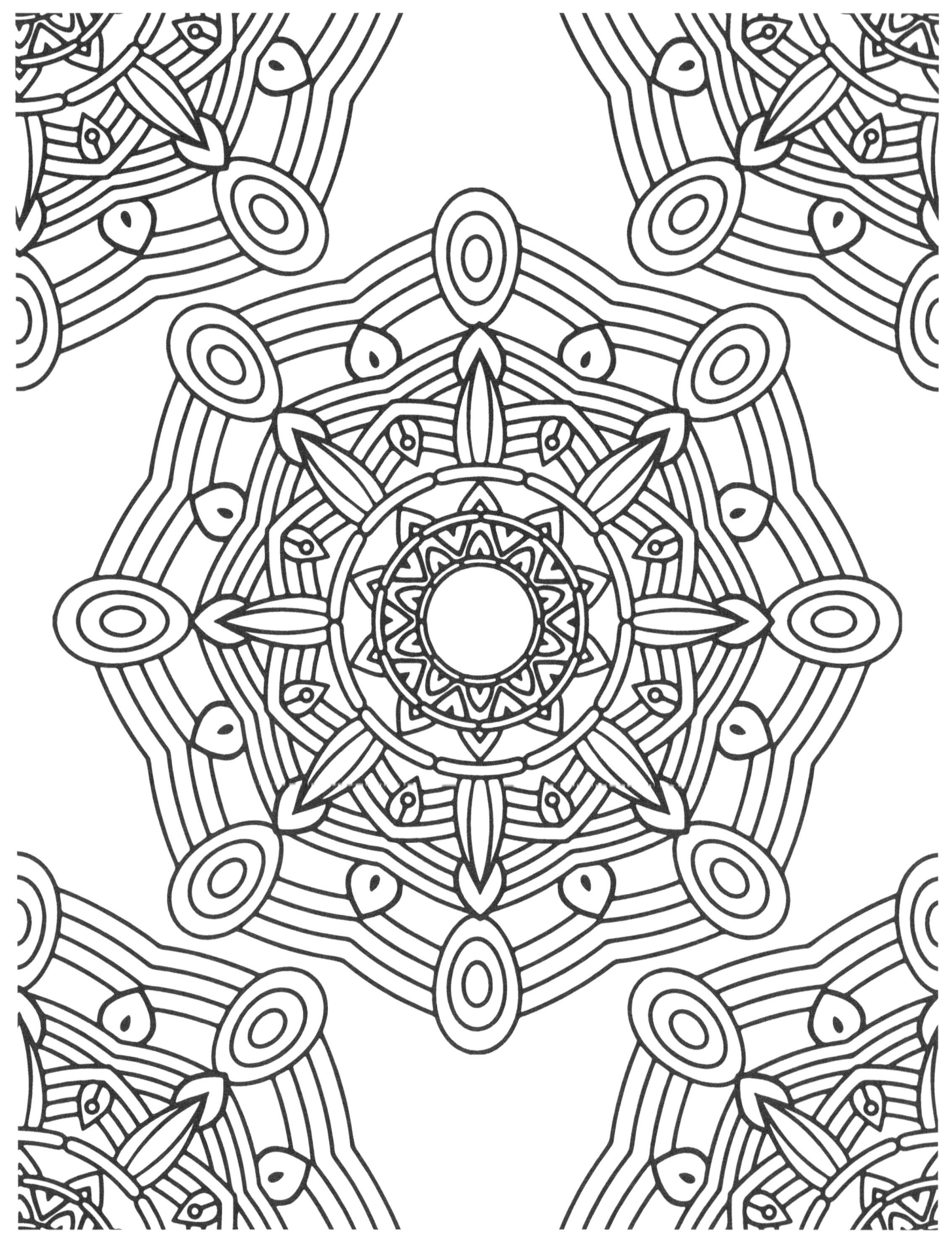

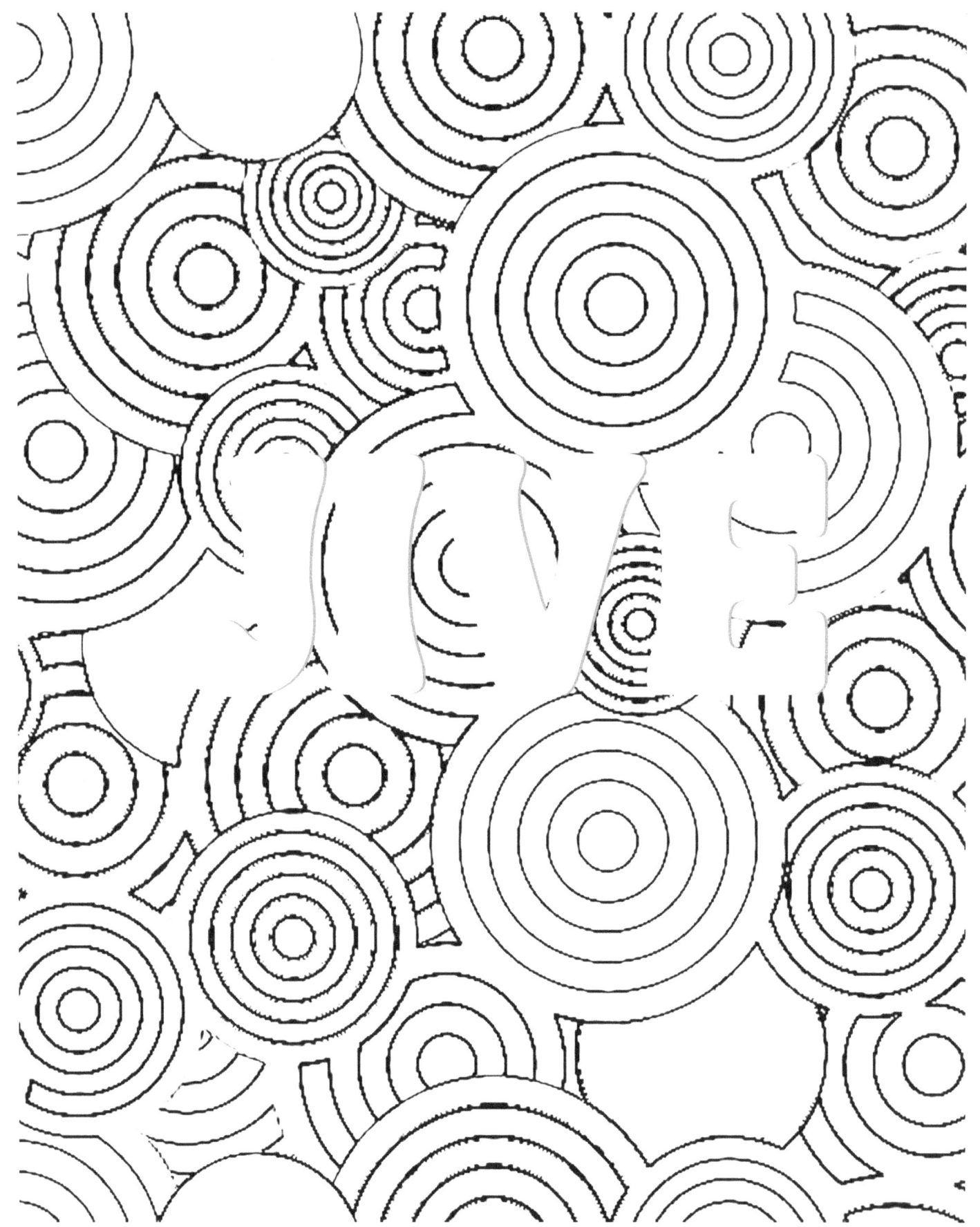

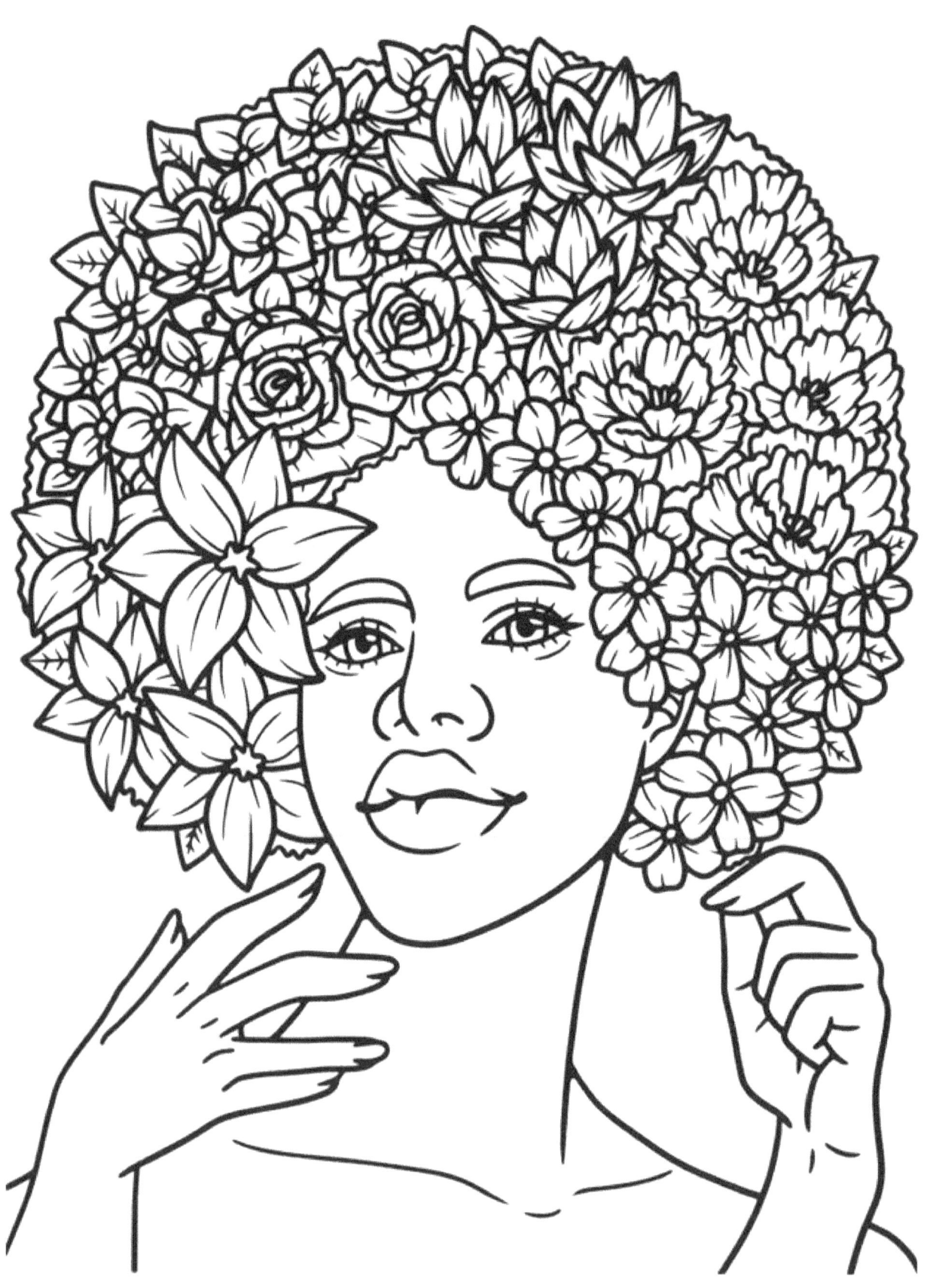

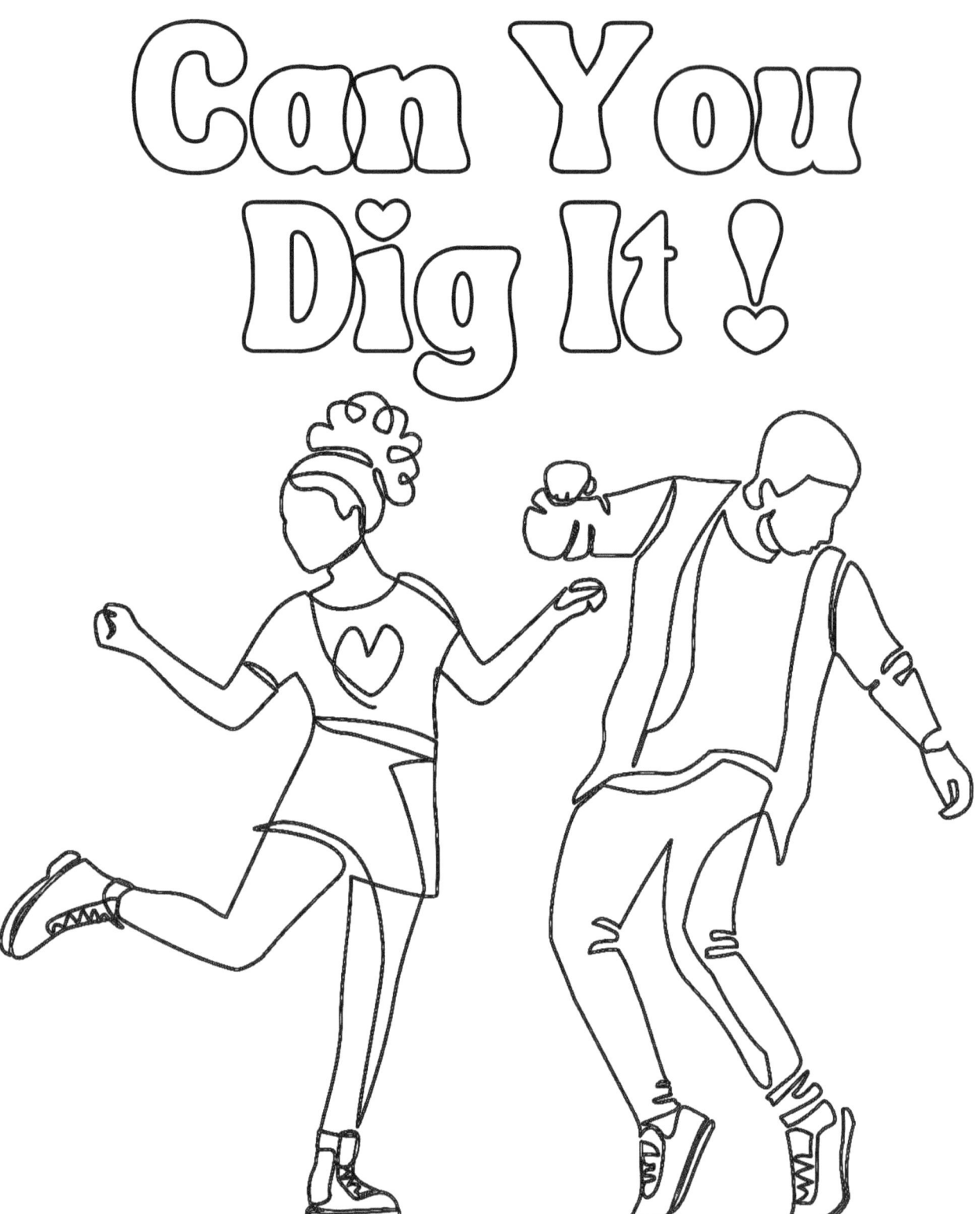

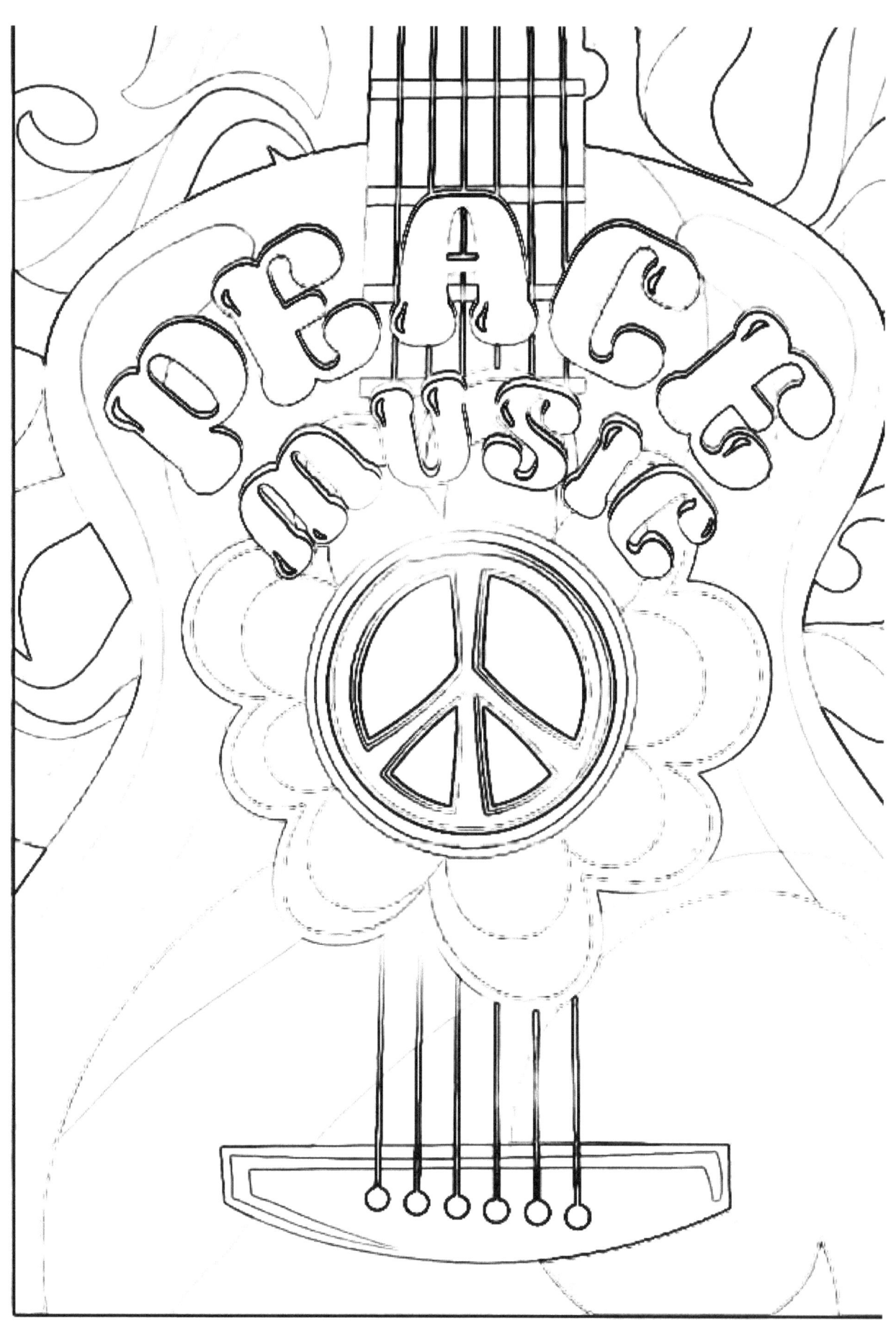

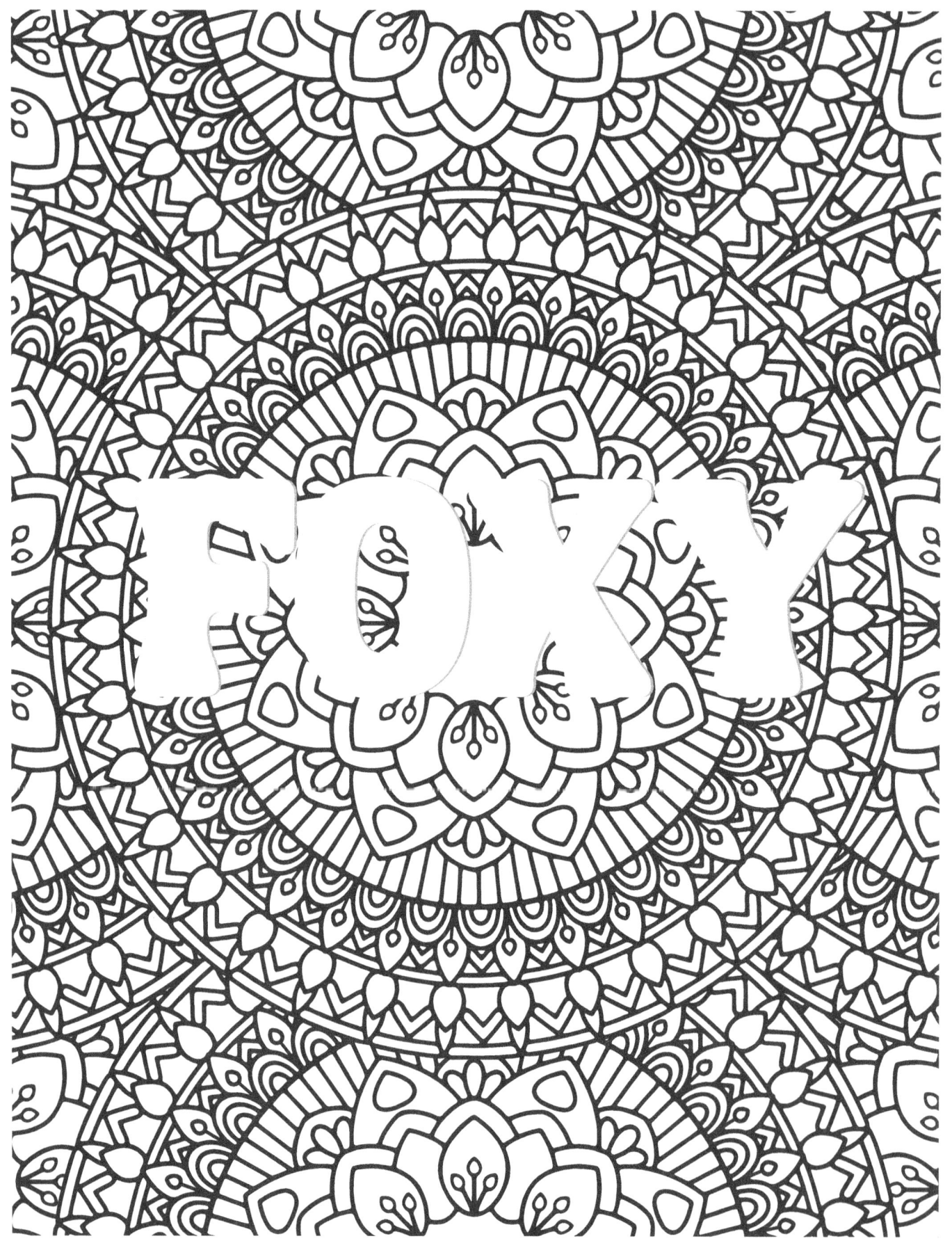

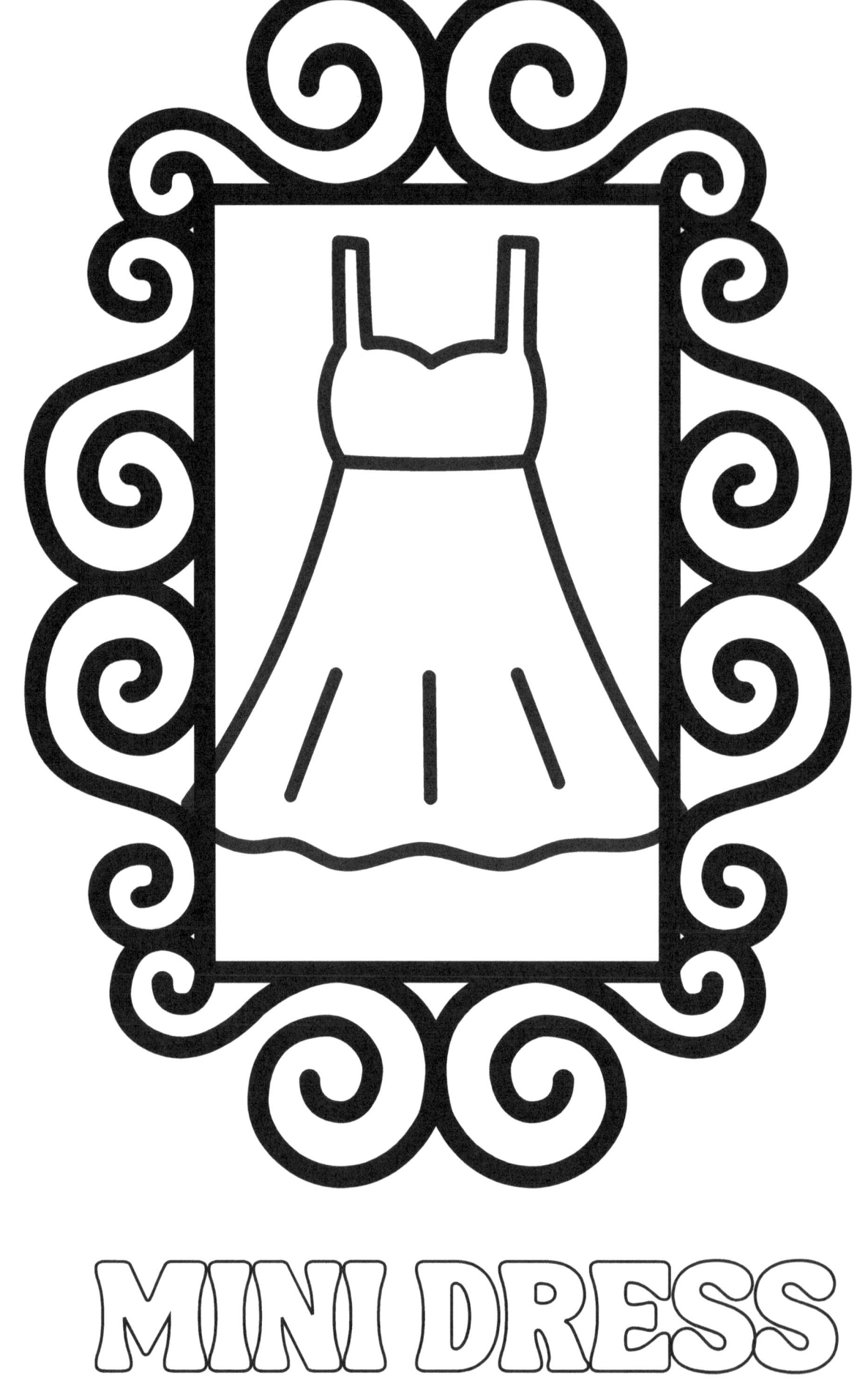

MINI DRESS

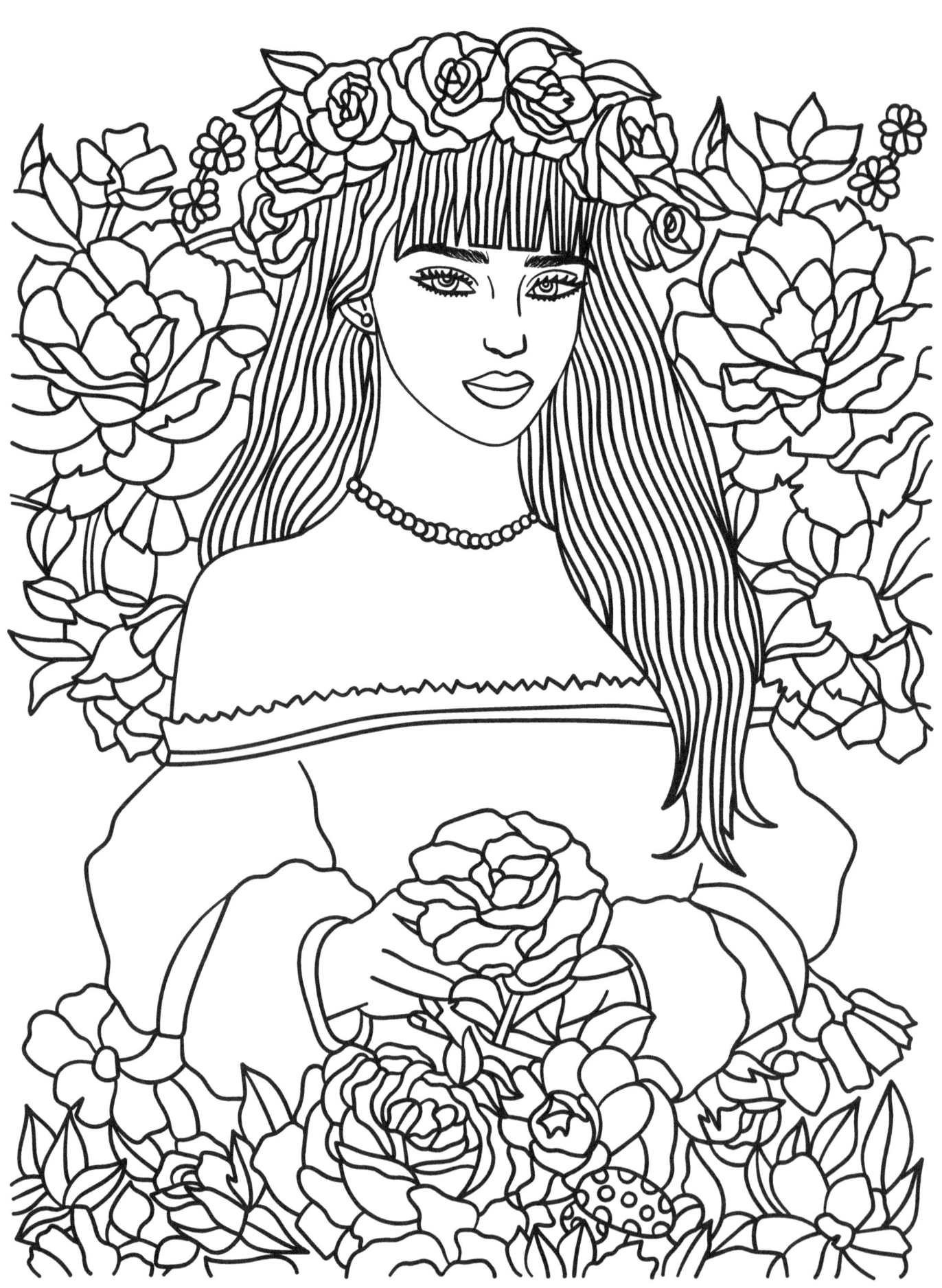

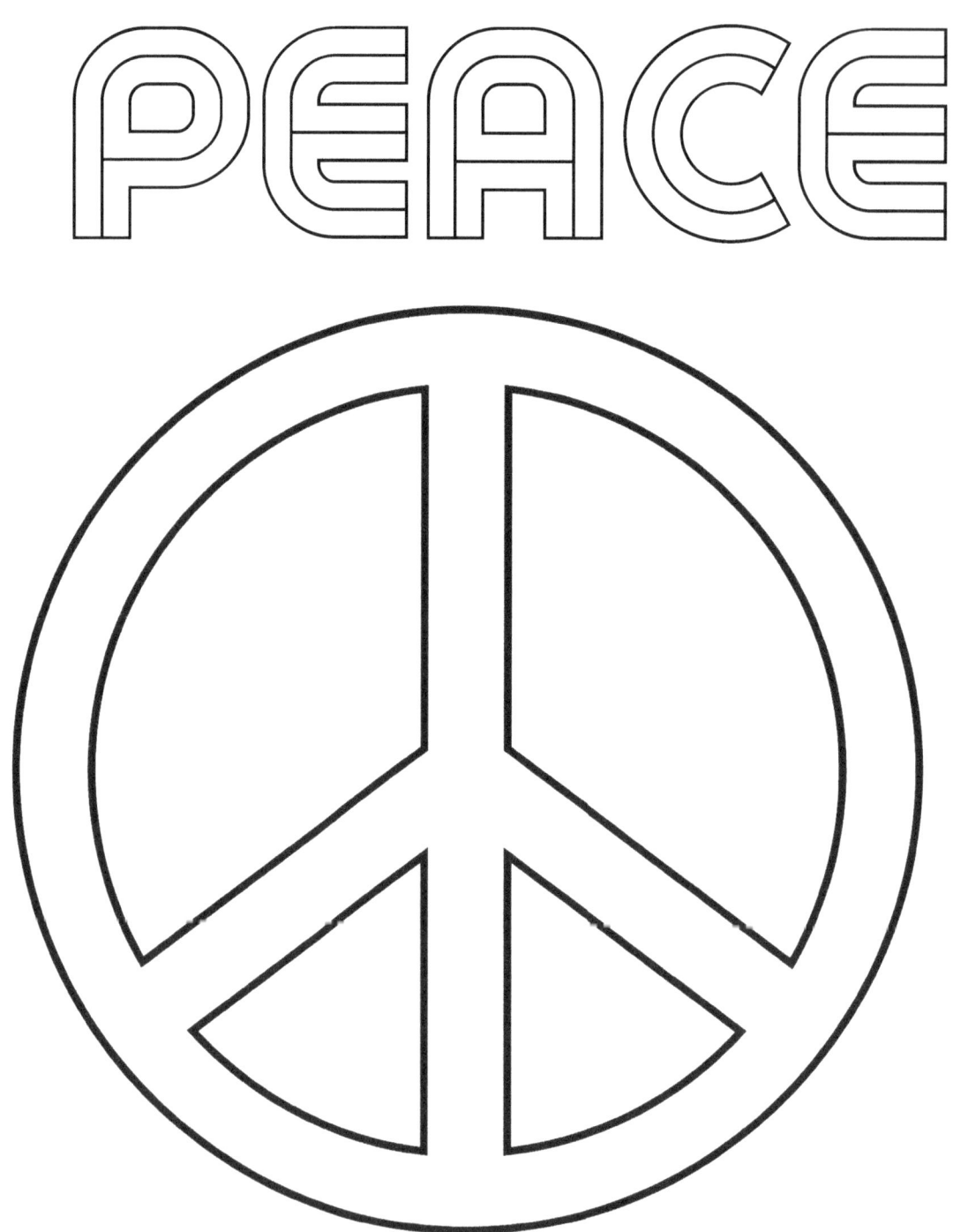

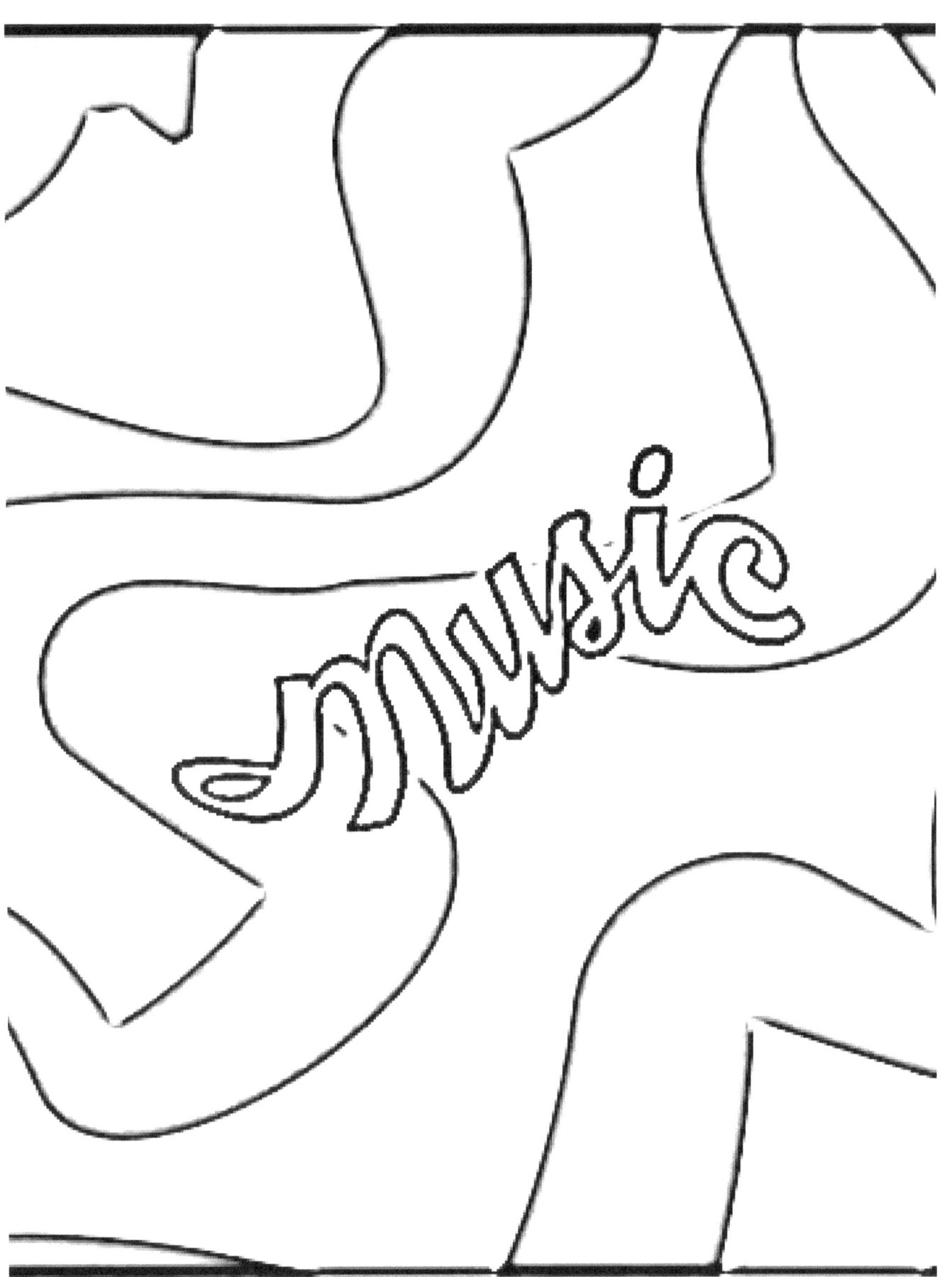

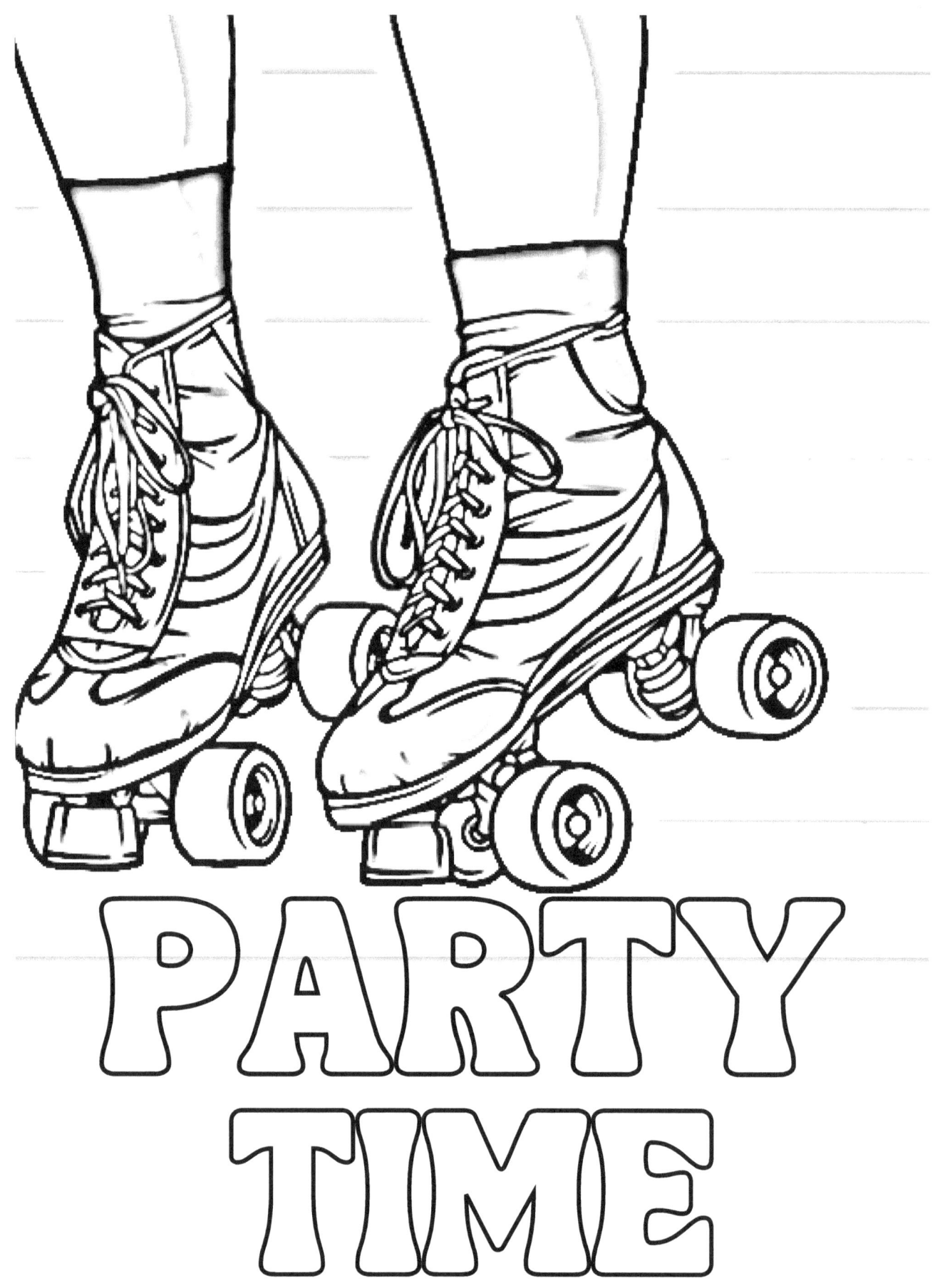

HIPPIE

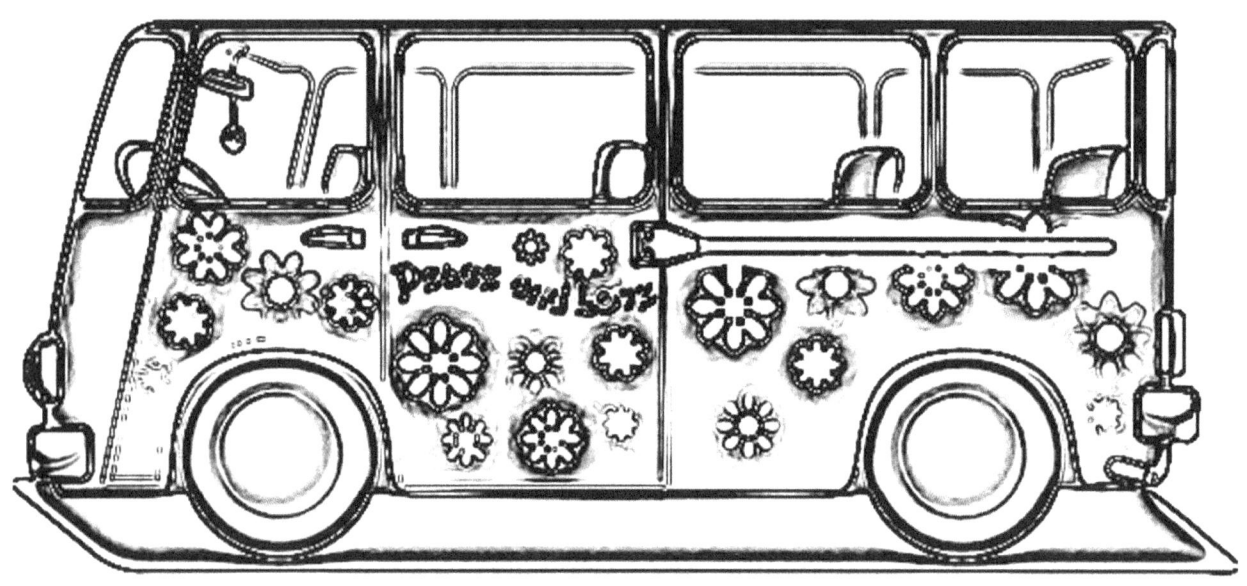

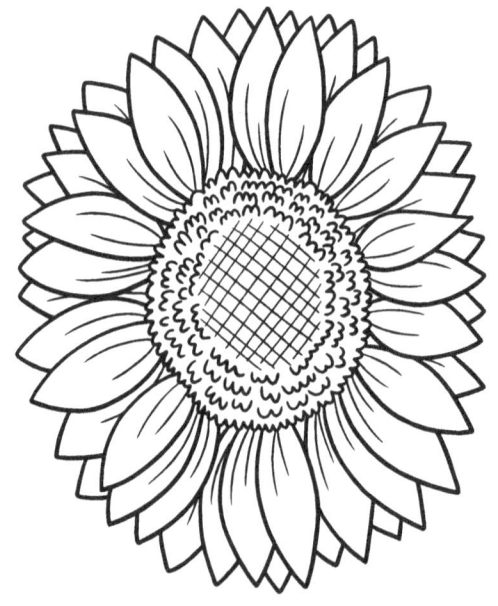

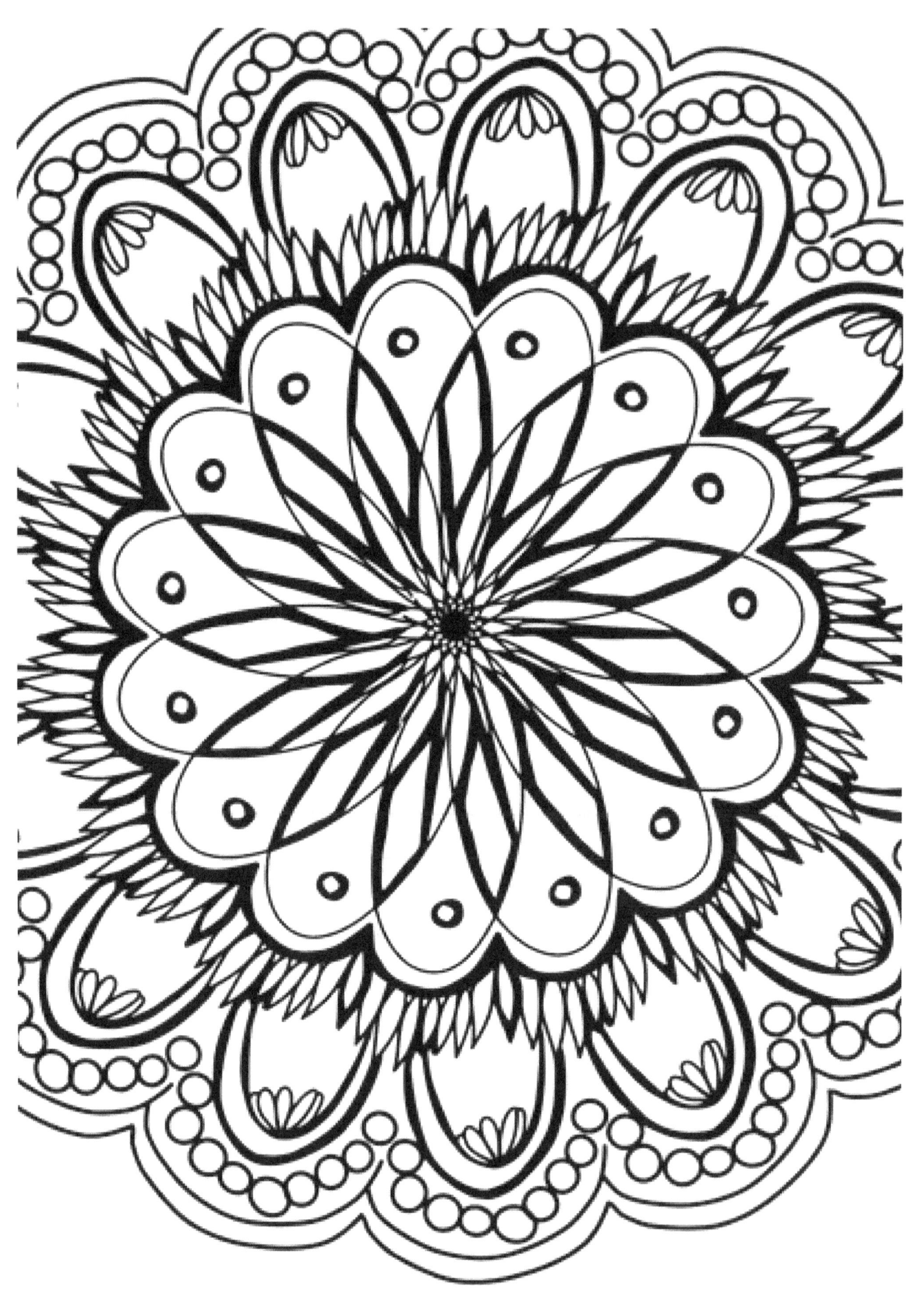

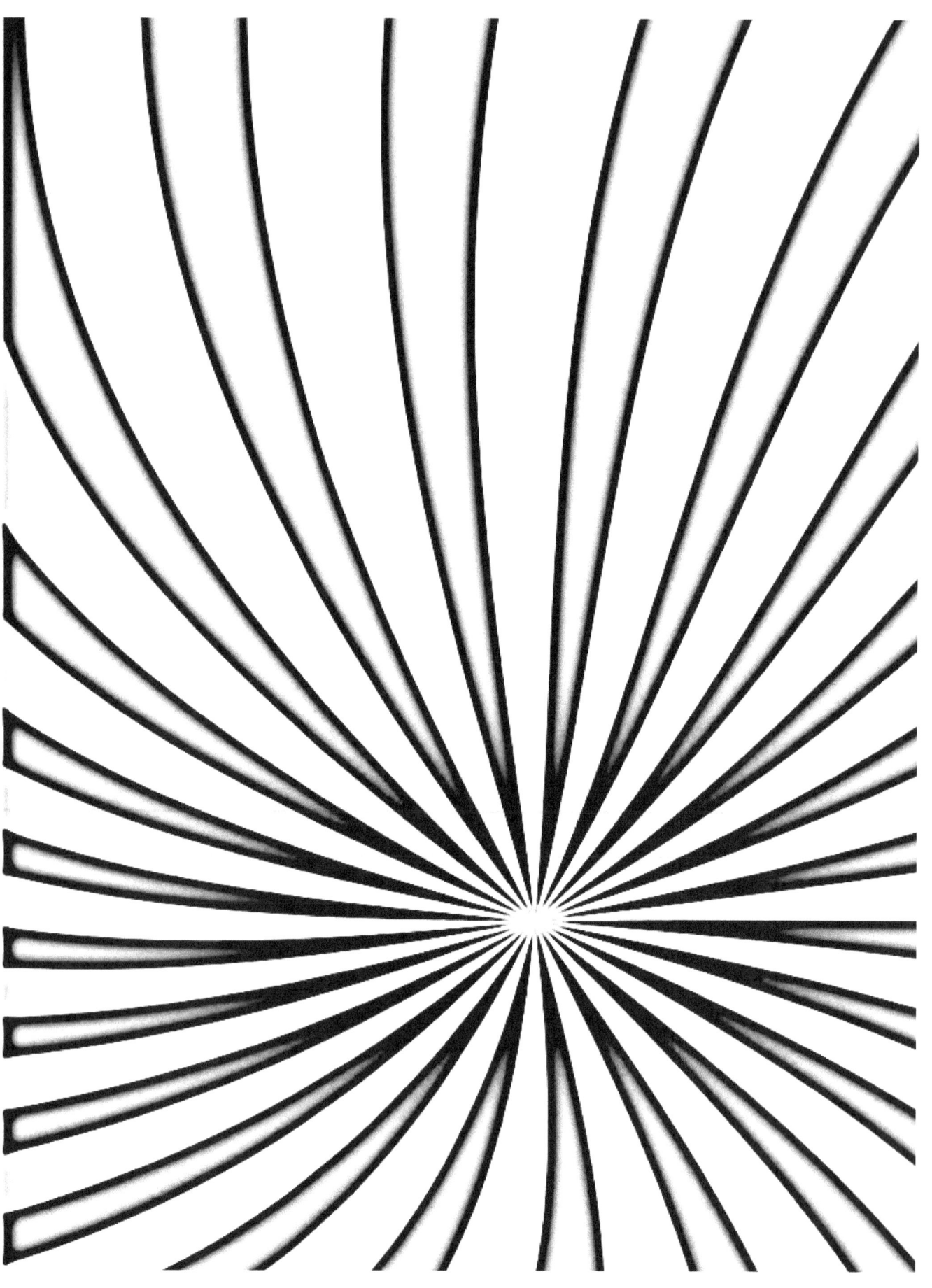

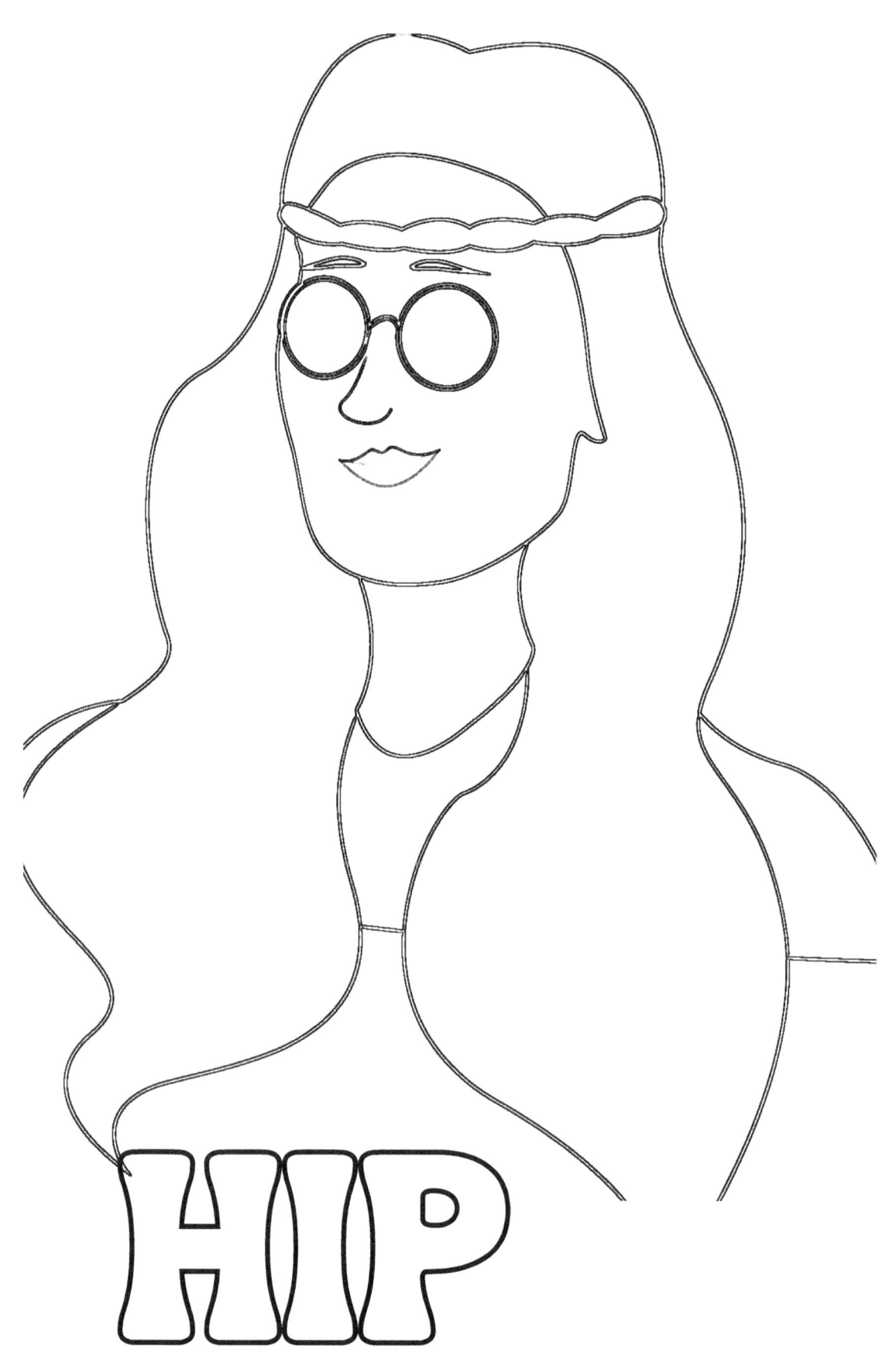

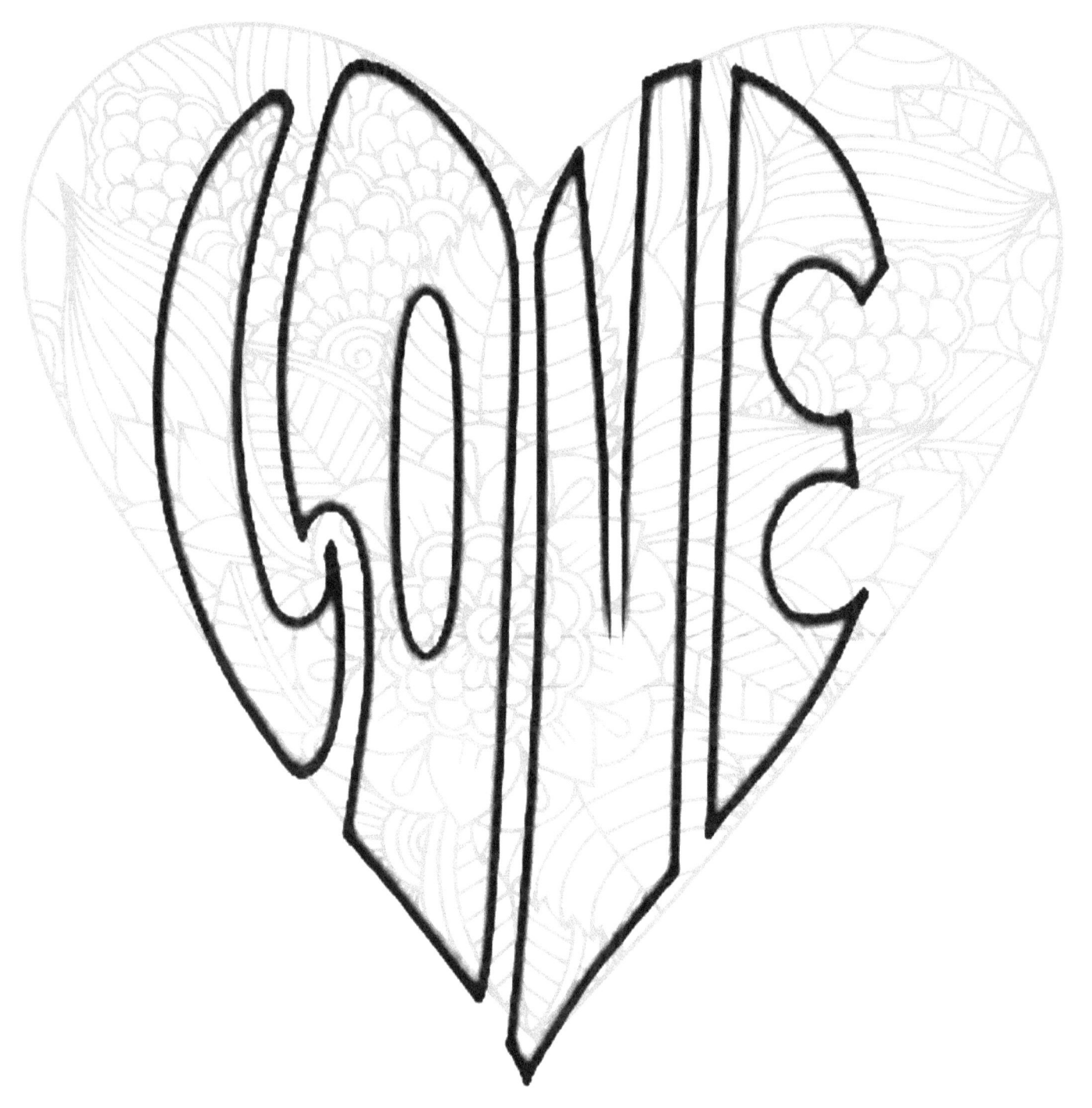

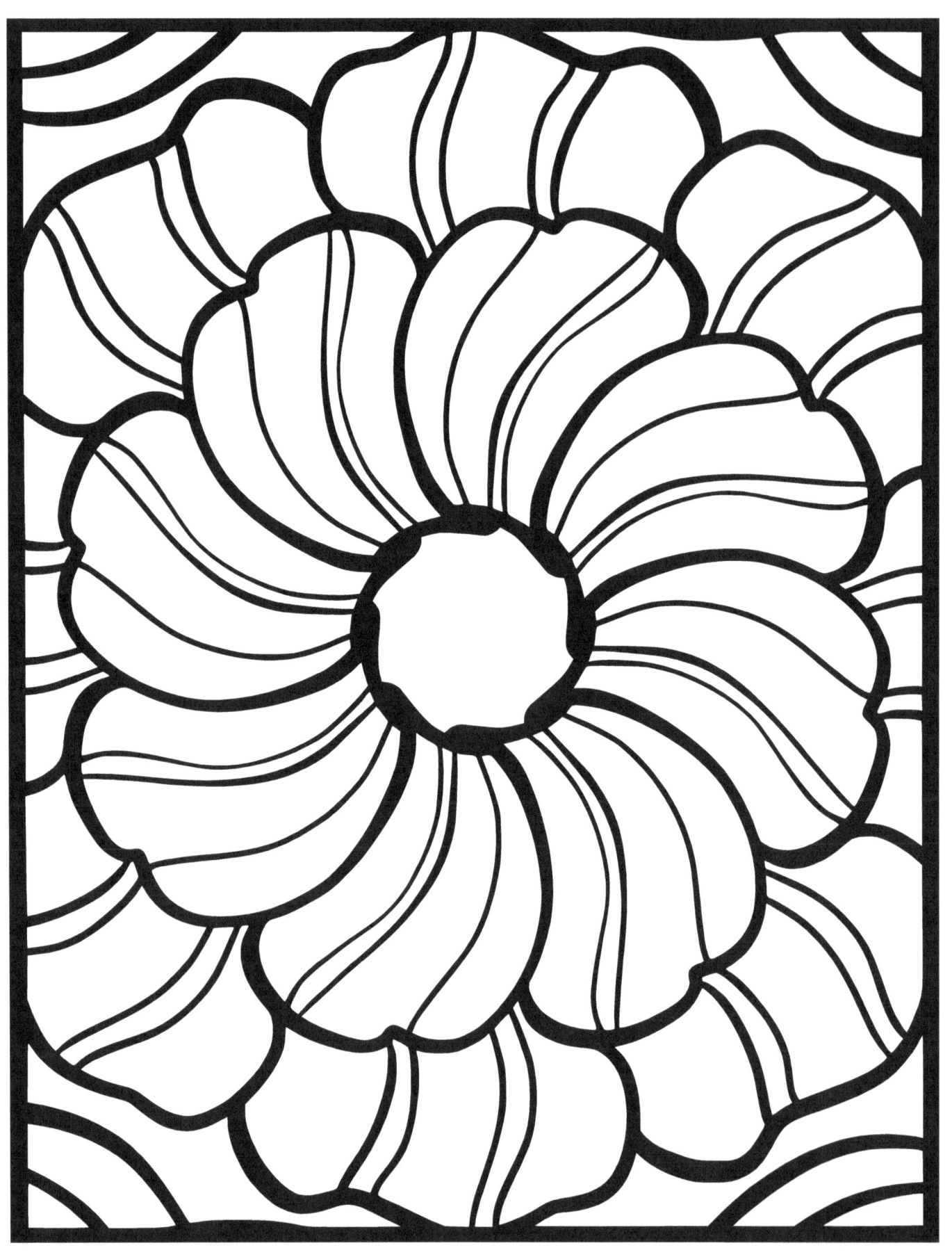

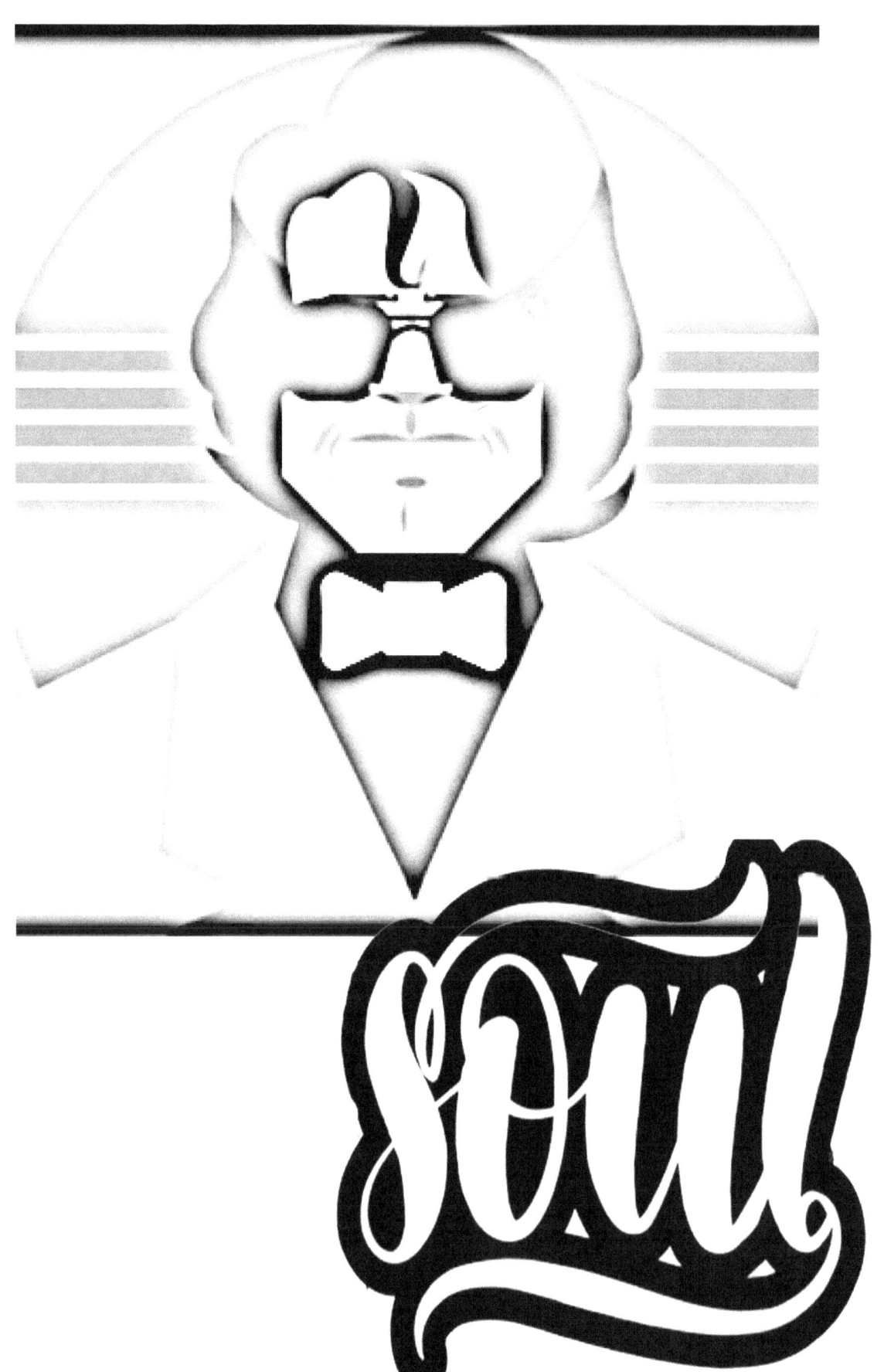

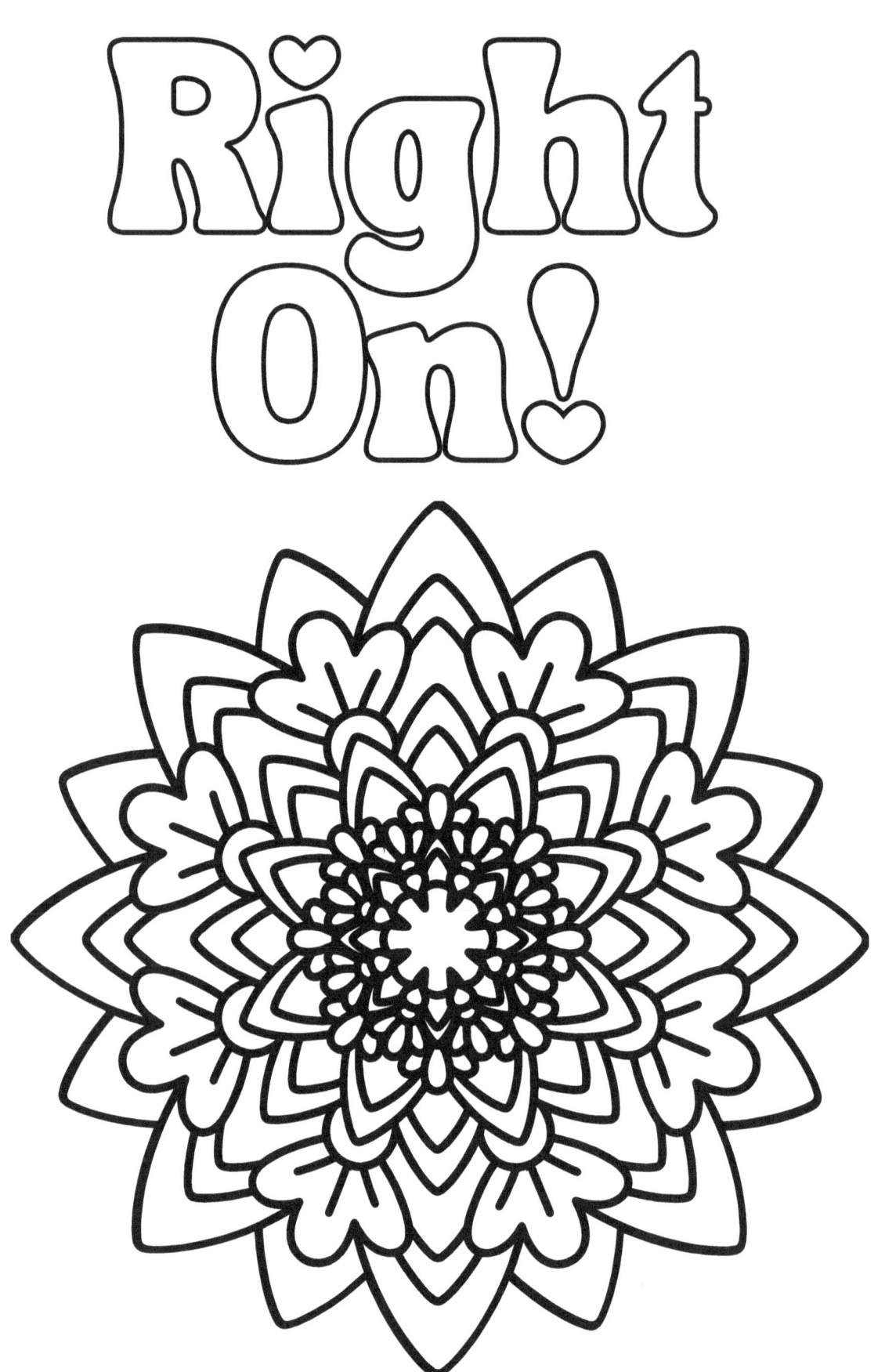

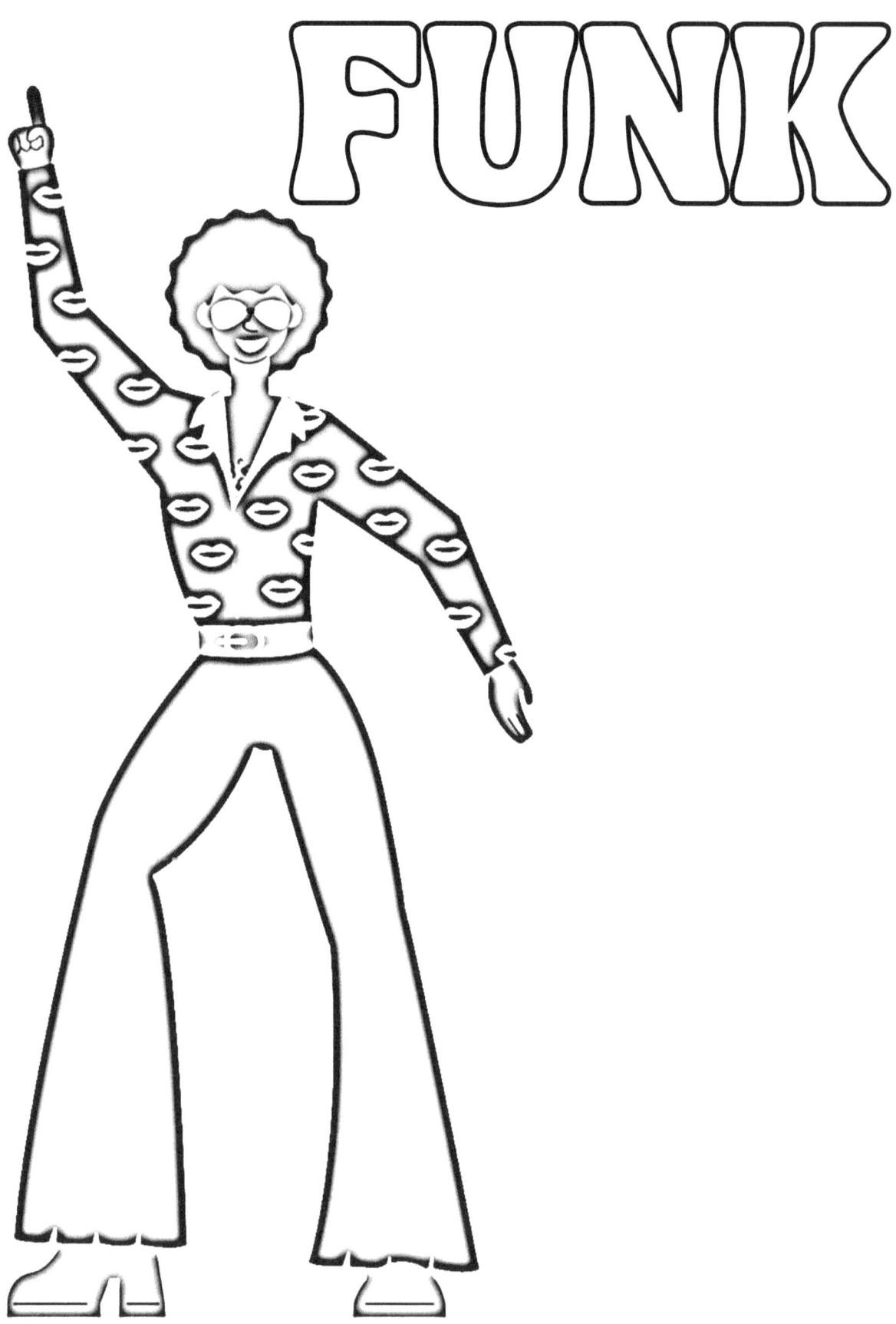

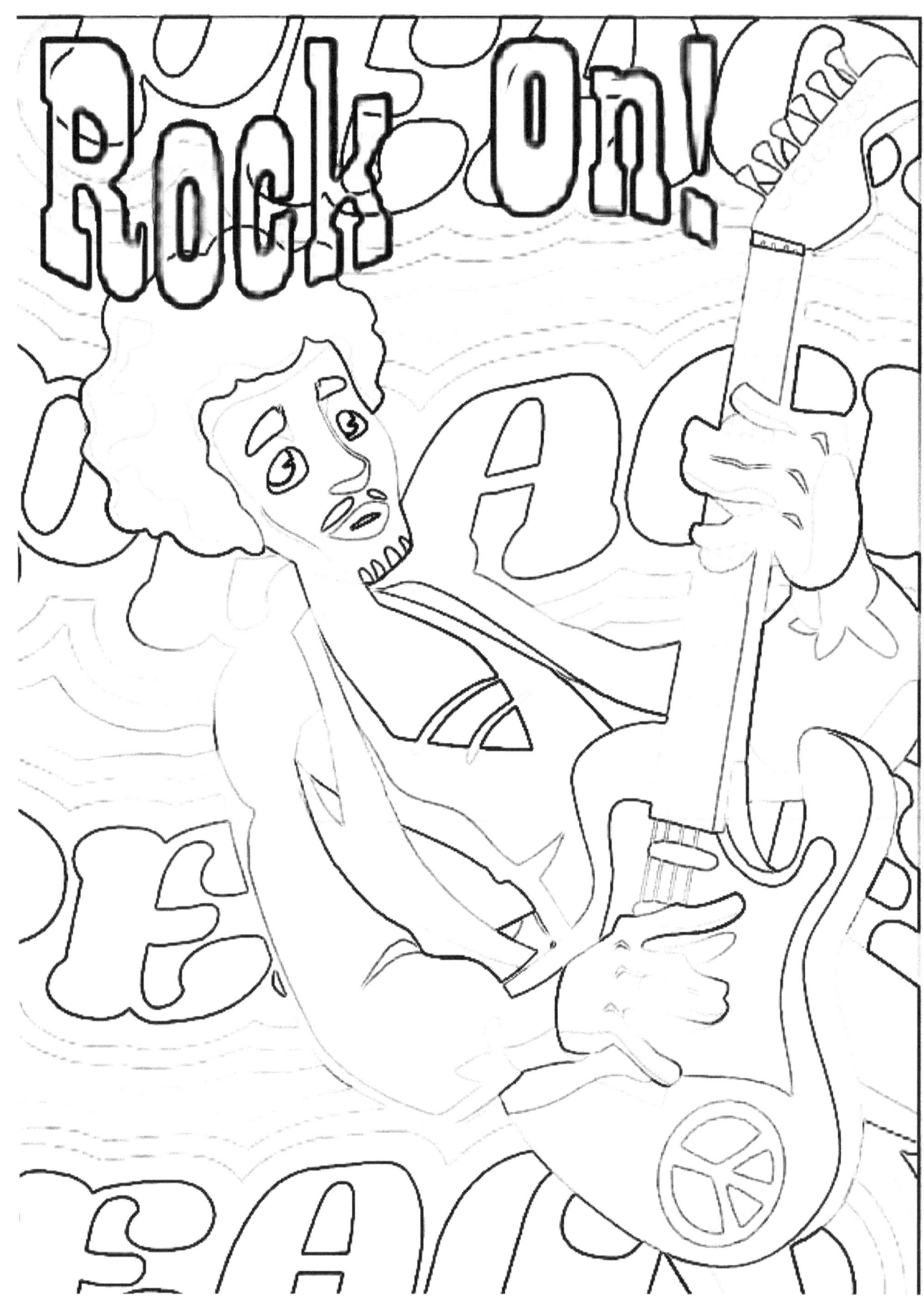

Boogie DOWN

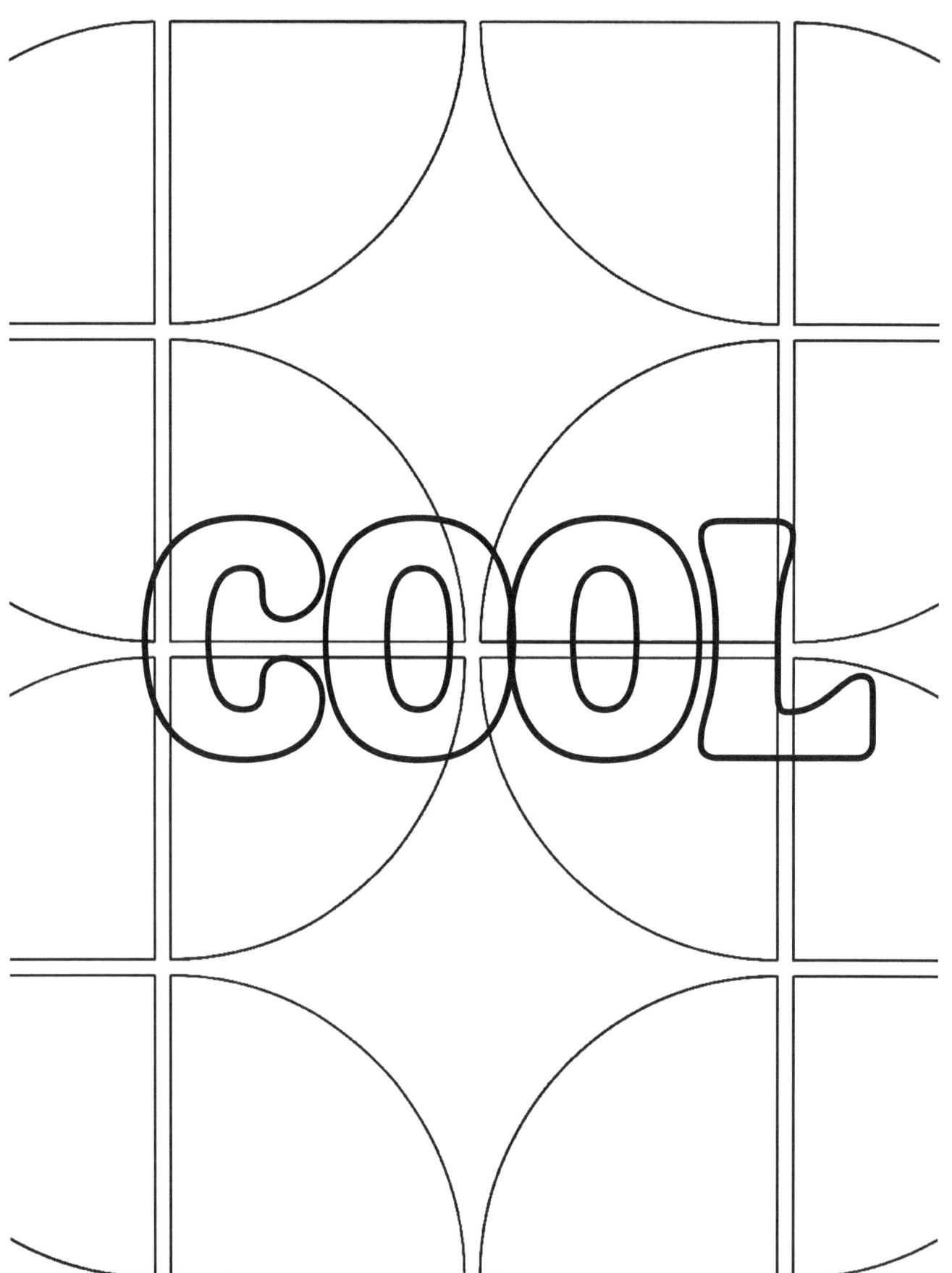

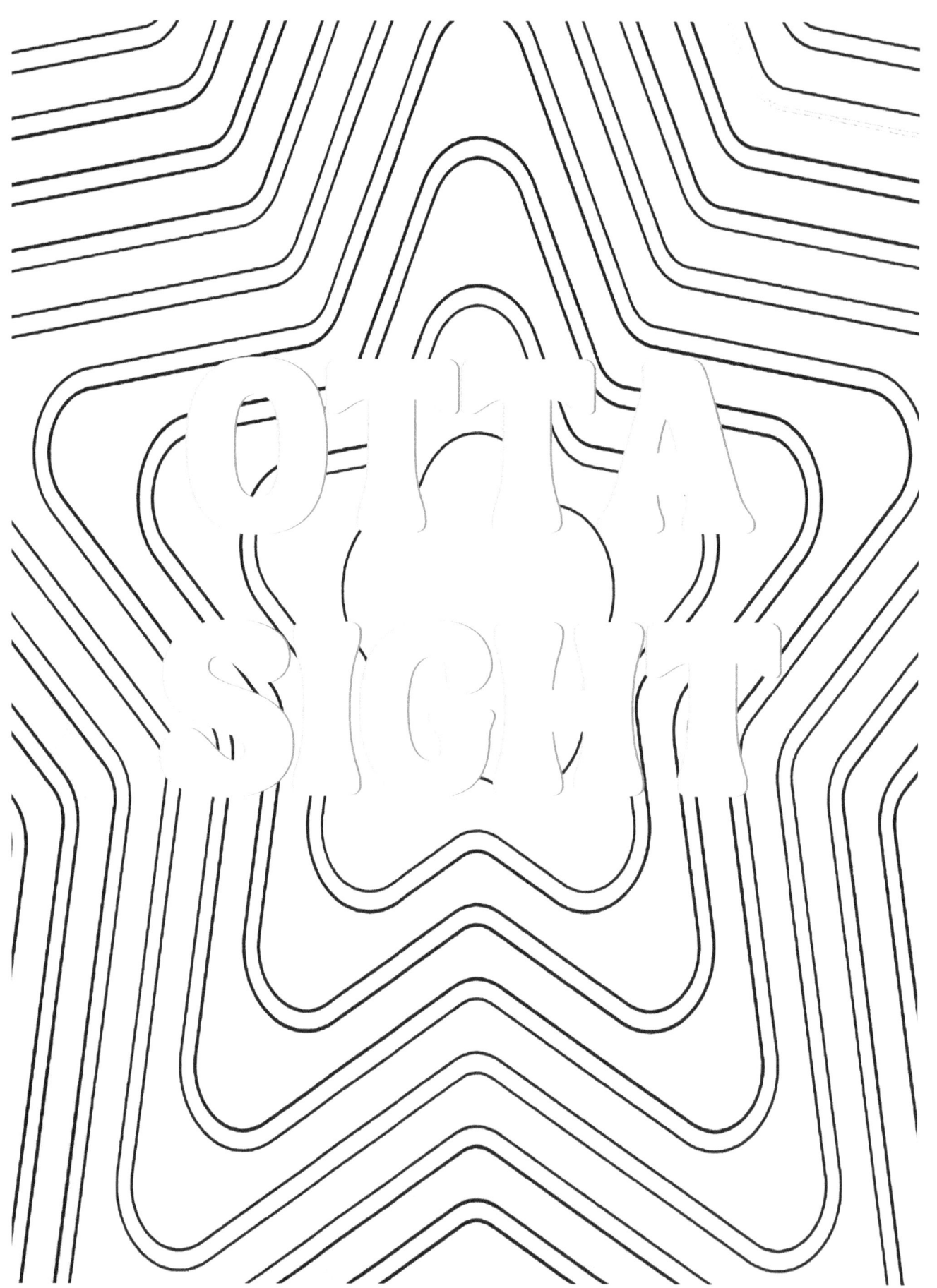

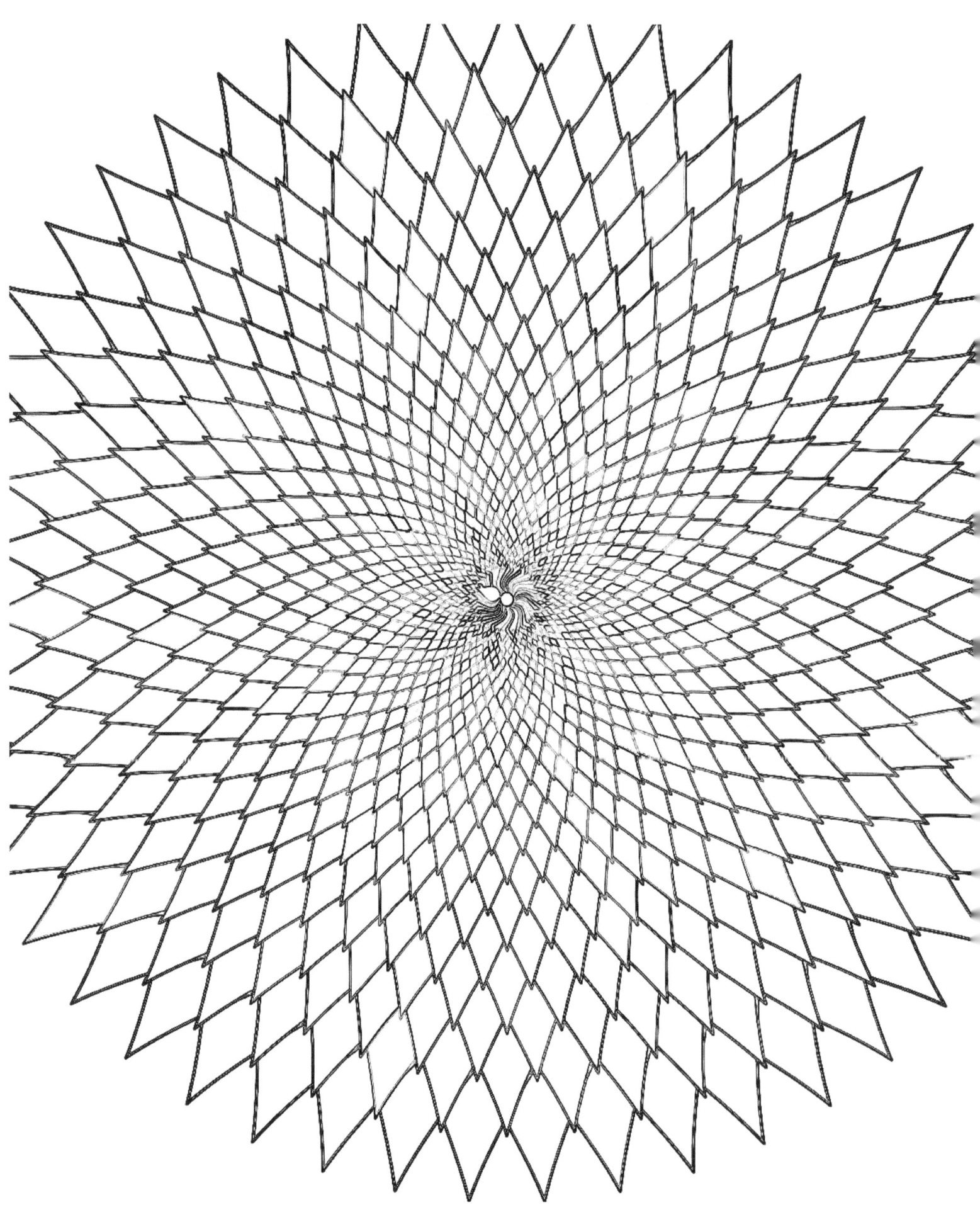

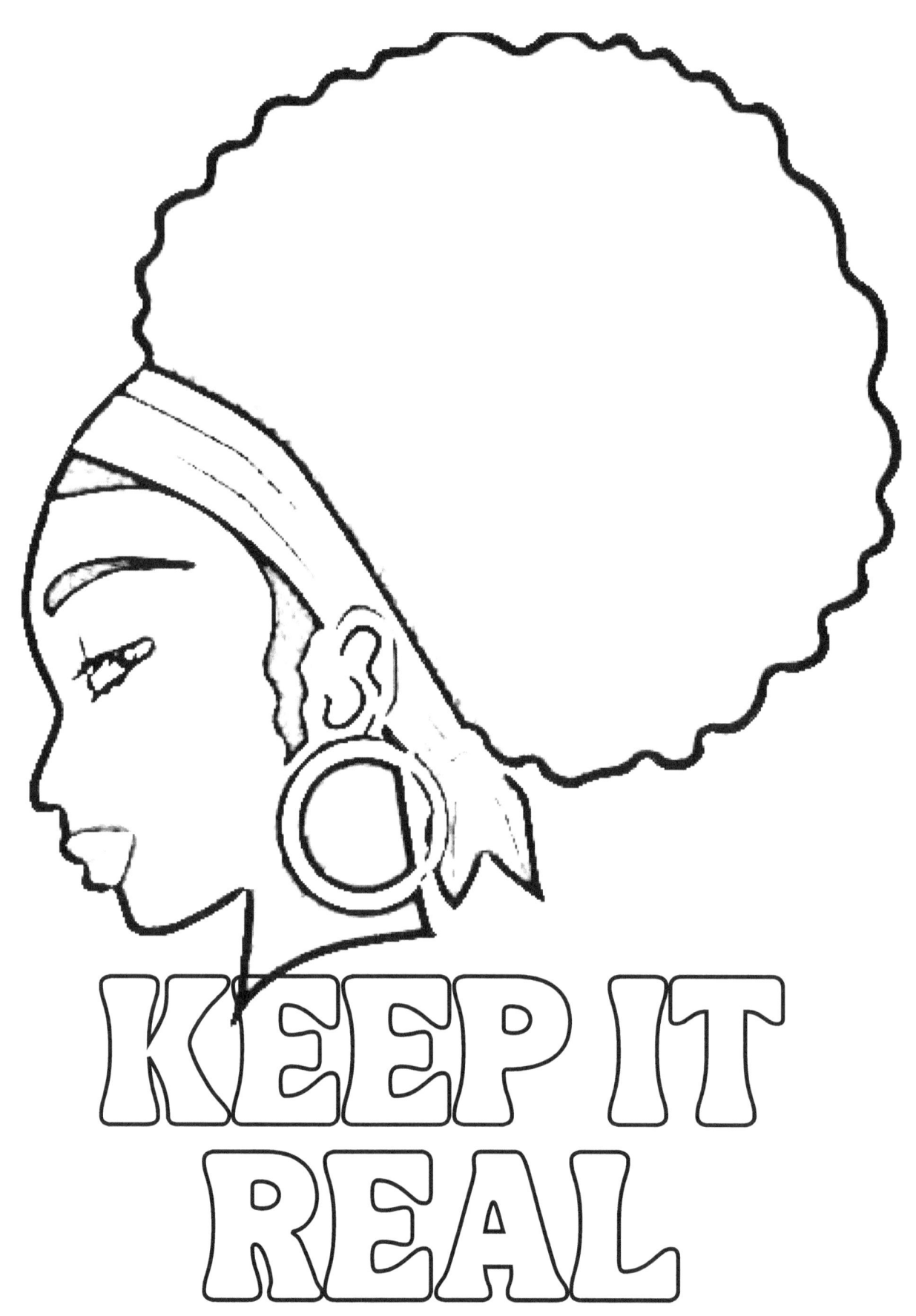

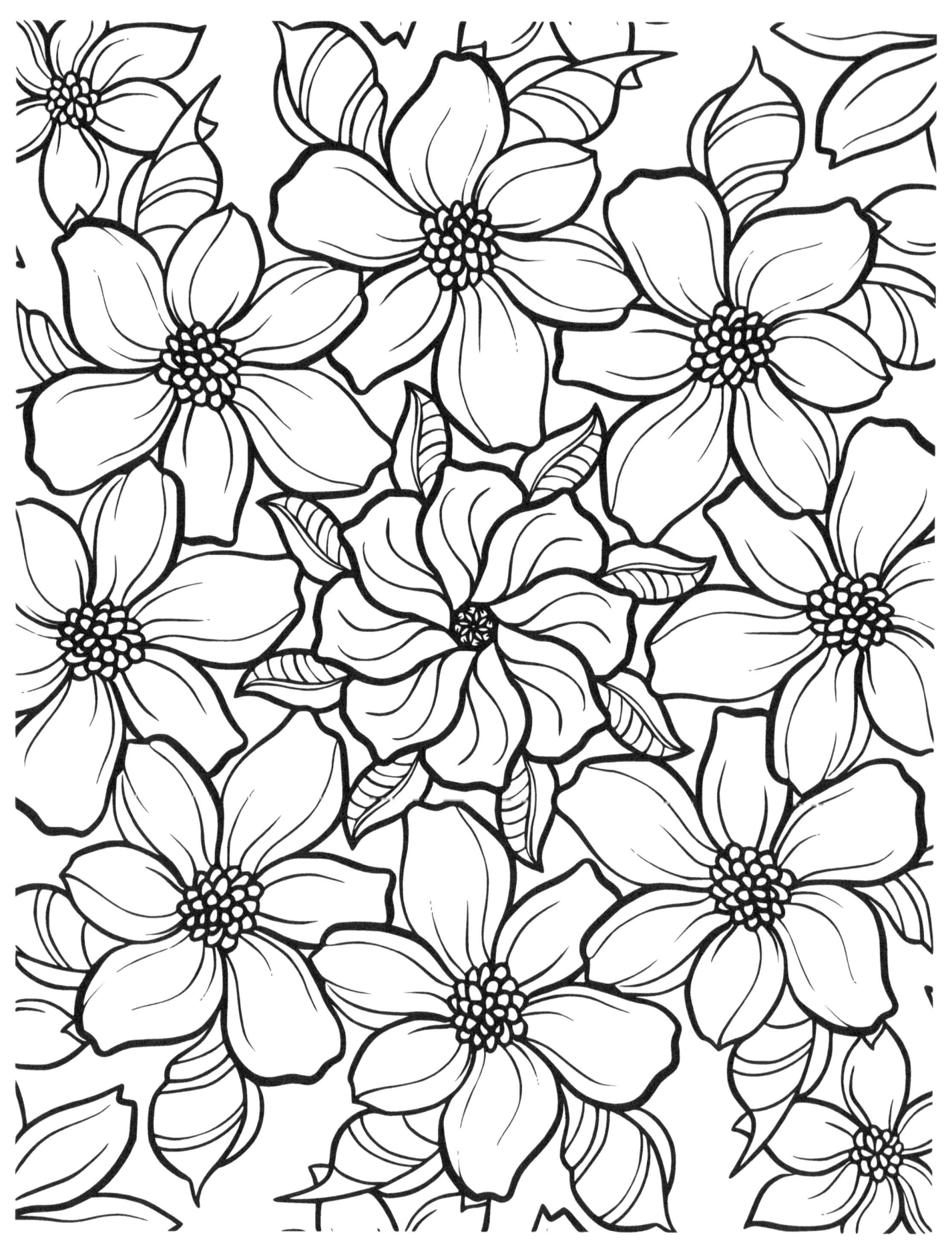

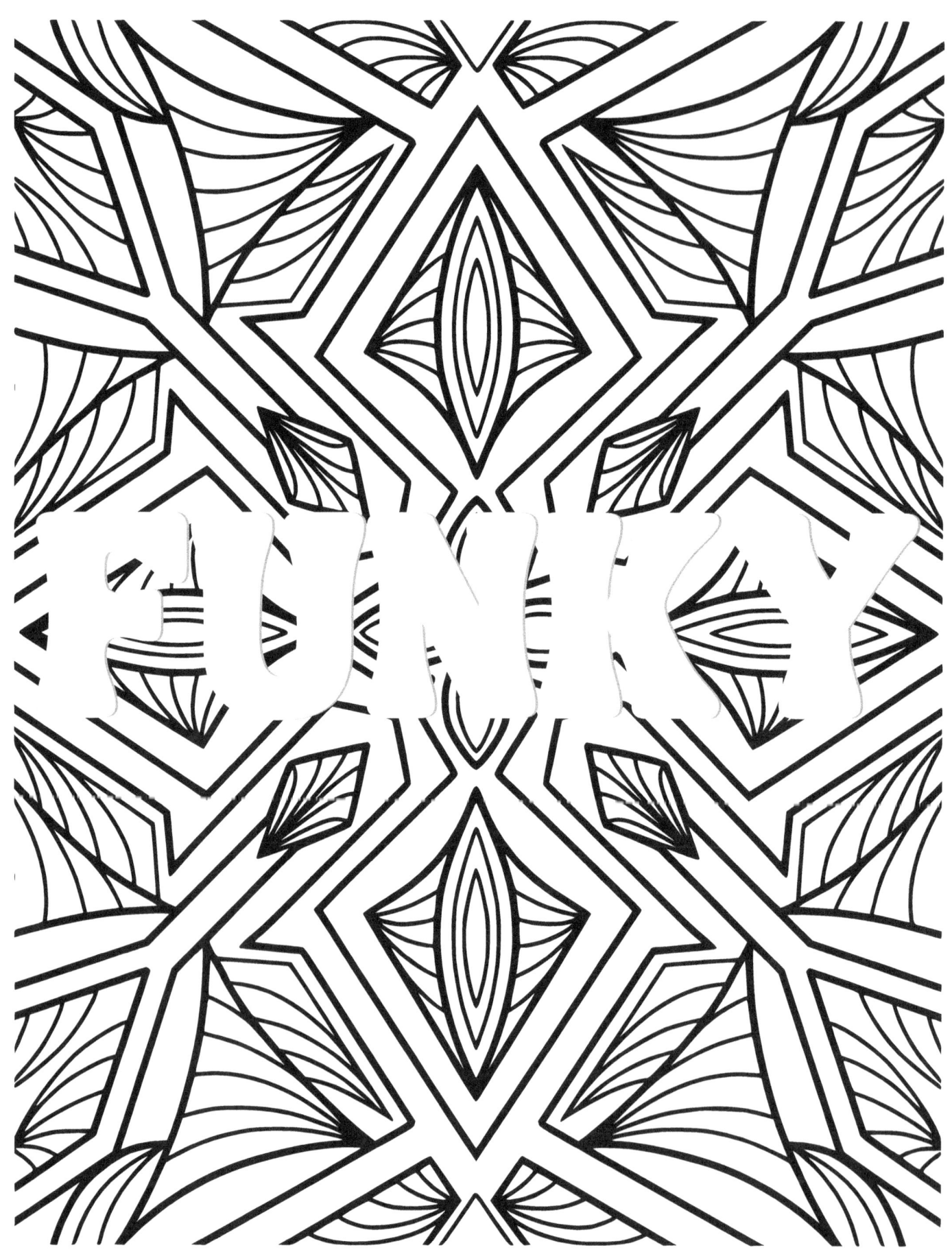

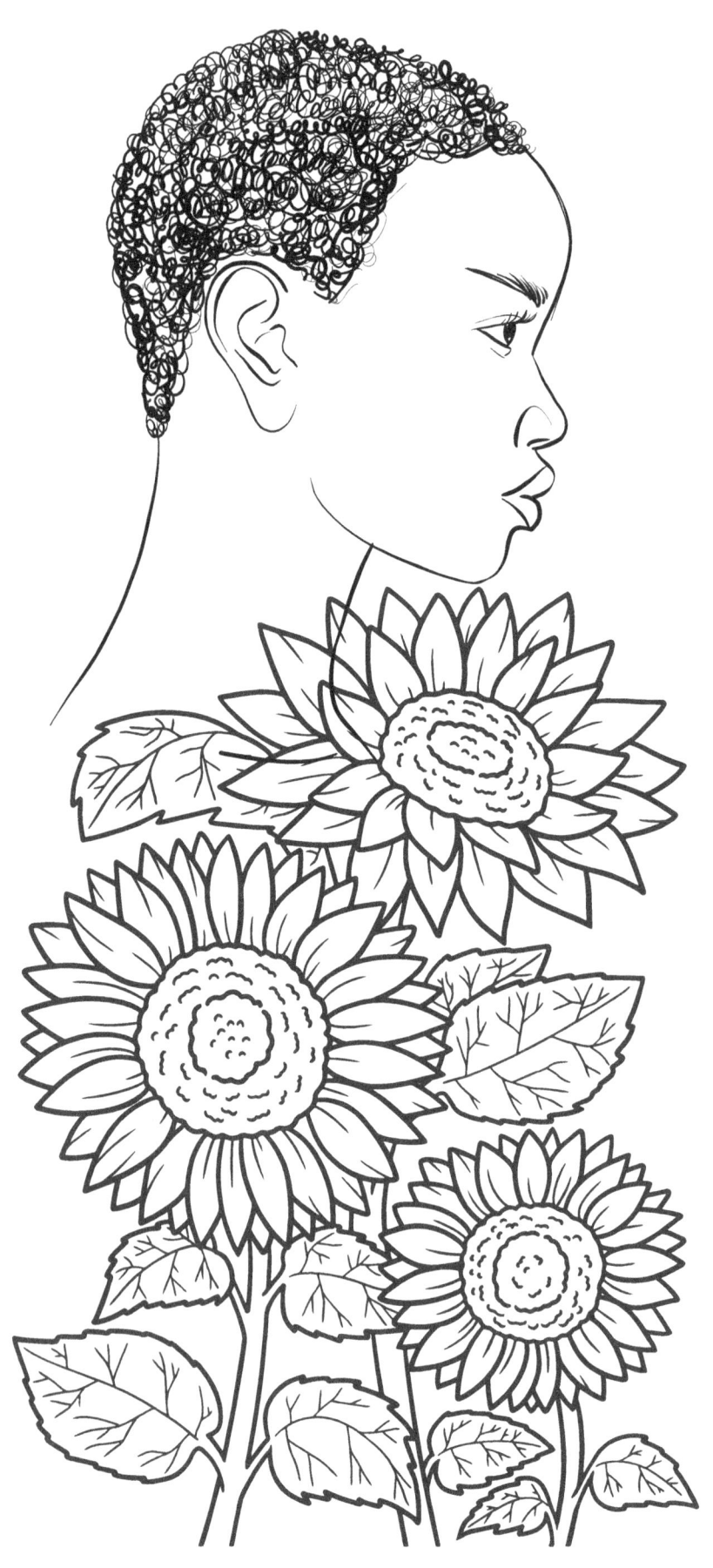

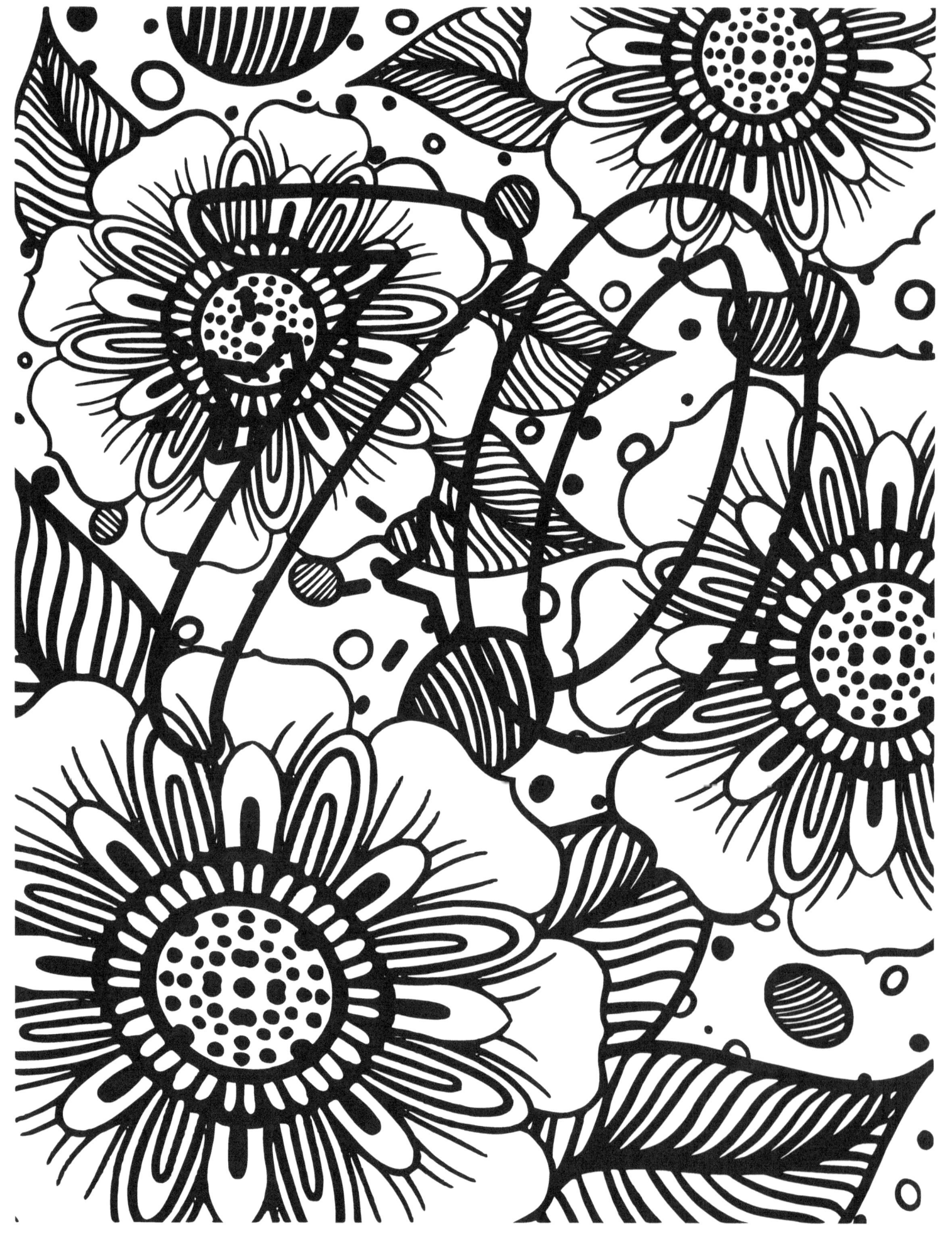

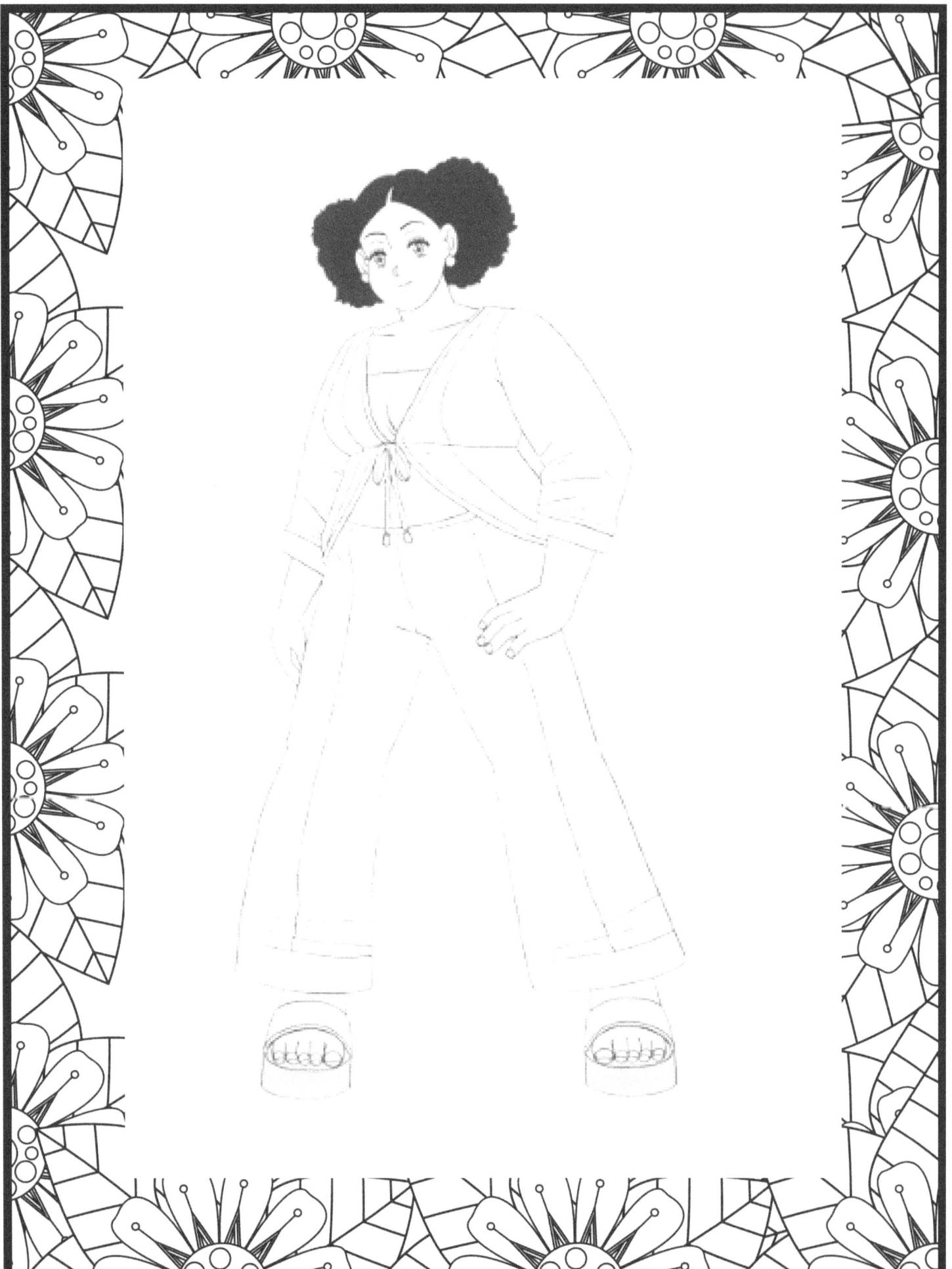

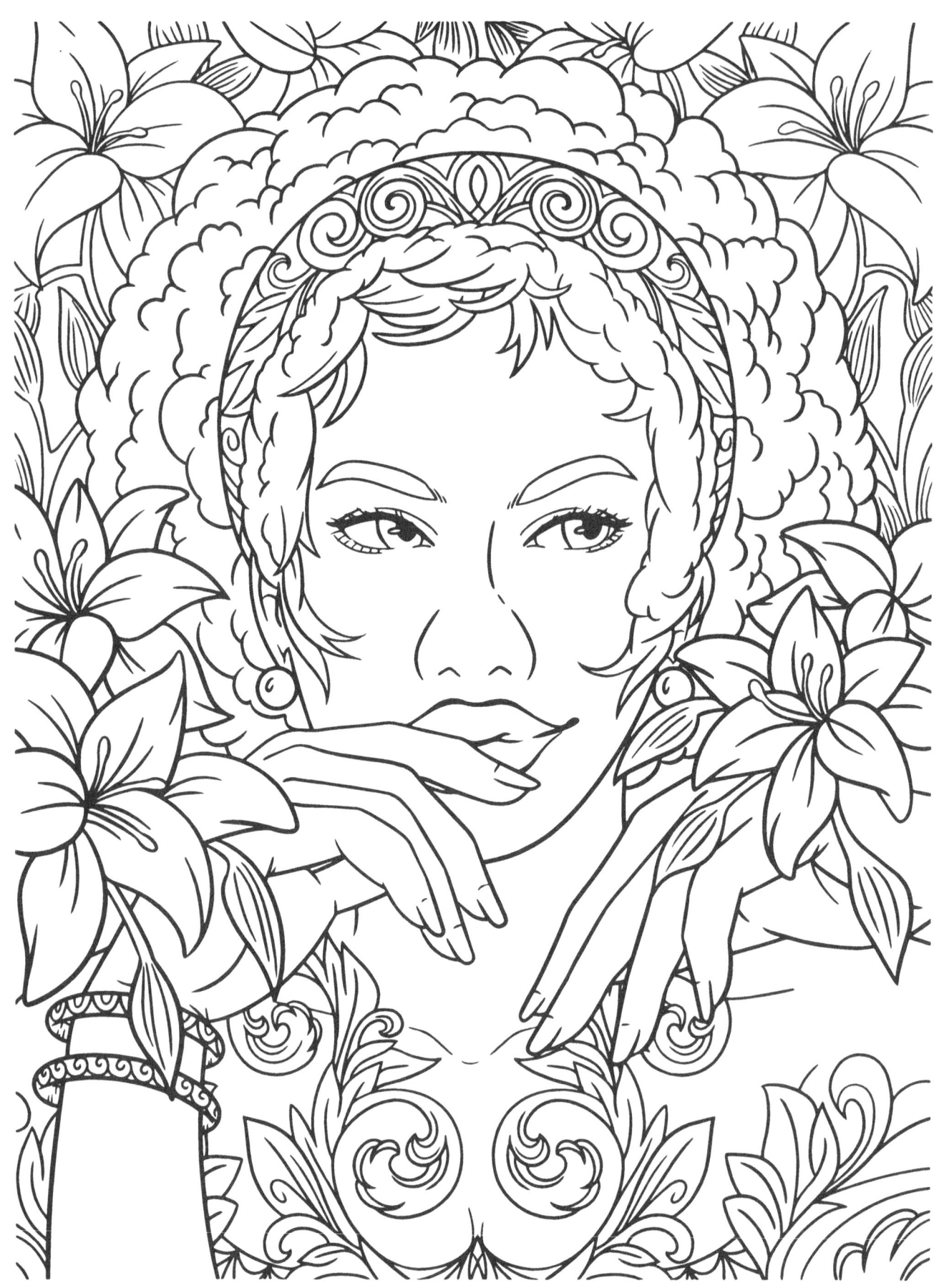

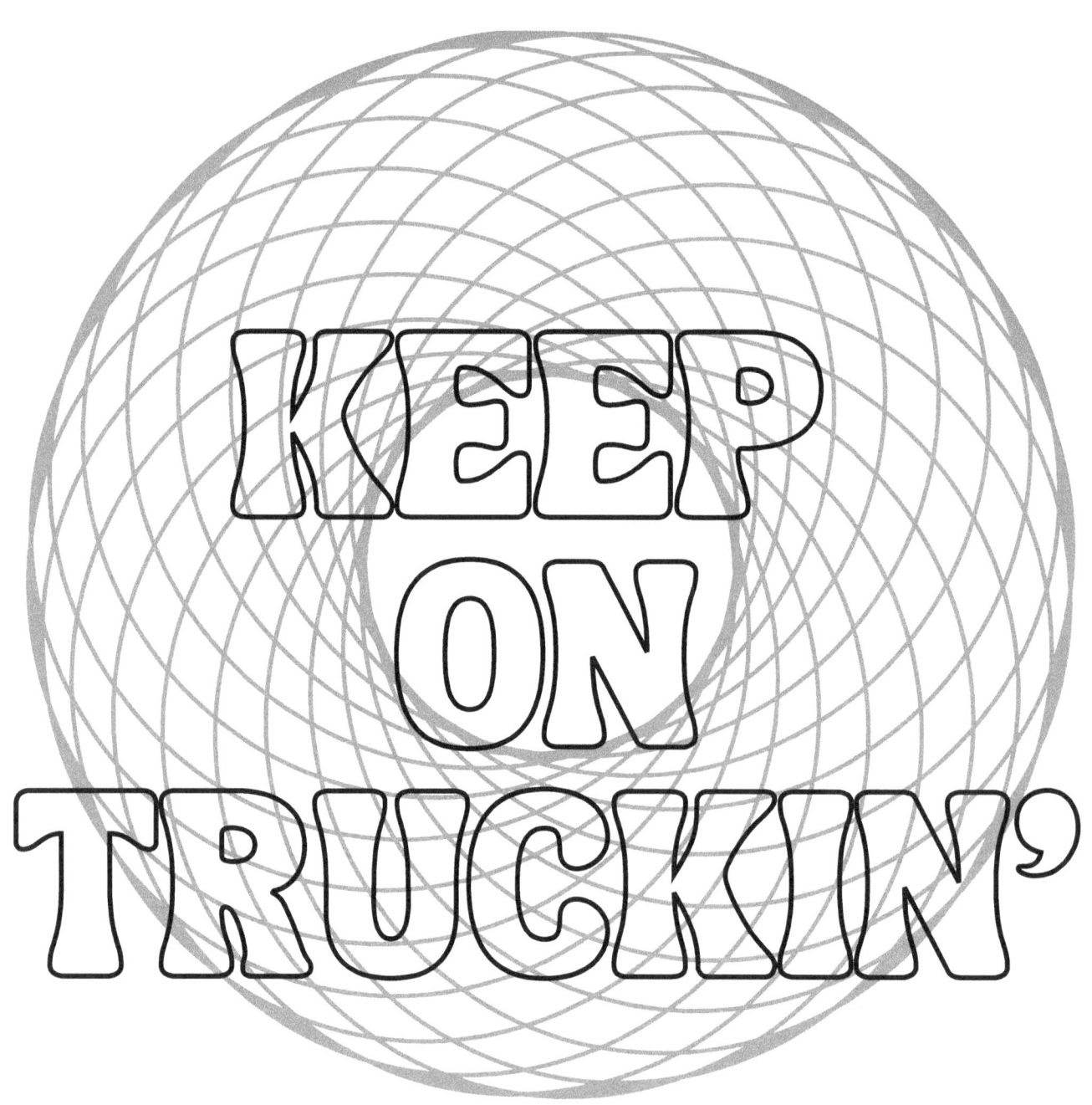

www.ingramcontent.com/pod-product-compliance
Lightning Source LLC
Chambersburg PA
CBHW080510220526
45465CB00006B/2436